HEAR THE SOUND OF TRUMPENCE

2

Hear the Sound of Trumpence

Copyright © 2019 Tonisha Fortune

All publishing rights belong to Tonisha Fortune

All rights reserved.

KJV version and ESV Version of the Bible used as reference.

All permissions and rights have been and must be attained.

TABLE OF CONTENTS

Dedication

To the Lord and Savior of my life, Jesus Christ. I dedicate this book to you as a token of my faith, as I dedicate myself to you, the Author and Finisher of my faith. As I watch out for your Return, I pray to you for this entire world. As the Remnant, a beckon of Light, I thank you for your living, dying, and rising. In a dark world, full of evil, we have hope in you to beat every demon. Knowing that we are more than Overcomers, we pave the way for your Second Coming. I love you Lord, and I give you all of the glory and praise in Jesus Name. To my husband, Delgraco Fortune, I love you and thank you for your love and support. As we read the word together the union of our marriage is formed on the foundation of Christ, may God continue His perfect work in us and bless our family, as well as all of the families of the world.

Introduction

Voices of Light overshadowing the darkness of this world

As a Hand reaching down from the Heavens, cradling the world within the grasp of comfort. God sent His Son Christ Jesus, bridging the gap for us to cross over. Seeing the division of Our Nation, the splitting of a party within the House, we must consider the word of God. Every issue, and problem faced has a solution through God's good grace. We must choose humility, and submit to His will, and realize that we can't do this by ourselves. We need supernatural insight, and wisdom from above, and then this earth will flow with the abundancy of joy, peace, and love. Let no one deny the Lord, and He most certainly will not deny us.   Forgetting past laws of separation, let us all come together United. Especially in our government, we must remember that the Nations rest on Jesus Christ's Shoulders. Let us be that Beacon of Light, for all the world to see in the darkest of nights. Being the land of hope for all Nations, all the peoples of the earth are gathered collectively.   Shining brightly with rays of love, all the evil in this world will soon dry up. Being the salt of the earth, sprinkling graciously, flavoring the atmosphere with God's great taste. Let us make haste! Because, as in the days of Noah we are all carrying on like tomorrow is promised, but it is not. As we continue to live our lives daily, let us remember to live each day for Christ.

As Lightning flashes and the thunders roar, let the Children of God voices be heard. Let the mouths of babes proclaim the truth, and we must all share the Good News. I know, fake news is flowing through the media, but what is real is the only thing that matters. Our Savior is Coming back for us! Don't be caught like a deer in the headlights, none of us should be caught by surprise. So, we pray for this Administration, the President of the United States, and every Nation. We rejoice, because a New World is awakening, the birth of a Great Nation, with law and order directed by Our Father. Let no man be made proud, but the time has come for us all to realize. It is not about us, not our wills, but His will be done. So, let us do what Jesus taught us, walk as He walked, talk like He talked, and get to the Kingdom's work. We know that faith without works is dead, and it is past time to move ahead. The devil has ruled long enough, so we stand in righteousness to take back this world. Darkness flees when the Lights come on, as One Body in Christ, Our Light will encompass the whole wide world. Believe this! All things are possible, there is nothing stopping it.

Giving testimony as a Witness of Christ Jesus, chosen before the formation of this world, a messenger sent to share the Word. We must all come together in love, God bless America and the entire earth. "Hear the Sound of Trumpence", is sounding the alarm as a voice of insight, the blowing of the Horn, the Great Warning. The Word of God foregoing made alive and brought down to this generation with sword piercing revelations.

As the Body of Christ, His Church, we must come together as One, and Shine Our Lights. Exposing all Darkness, salting this world with His Love, because we are sanctified and covered in His Blood. We are Family, the Children of God. In Jesus Name, Amen. And, this book is an attempt to unite us all in One Body as the People under God in Christ. Though it might seem impossible, we believe that all things are possible with

Christ Jesus, and faith is the substance of what we hope for. Let us all have the Kingdom as promised as Our inheritance.

Let us come together for the good of ALL people, United in the Body of Christ we are unbeatable. We are a Chosen Race, a Royal Priesthood, a Holy Nation, a People for God's Own Possession, so we must proclaim His excellence as we are called out of darkness into His marvelous Light. He chose us in Him before the foundation of this world, therefore we are Holy and blameless before Him in Love, adopted as Sons and Daughters through Jesus Christ to Himself according to His will, not ours.

Chapter 1-

Lifting up the face of our Nation

First, allow me to salute President Donald Trump for his work on major issues that impact me personally, this is an effort to help the Nation move closer to the greater within our union. The Religious Liberty Executive order, called "Promoting Free Speech", as a writer and an advocate of Christ I stand with the voice of reason on One Accord with all the Saints, saying Jesus Christ is Lord, and there is no other Name by which we are saved on earth. Our voices will be heard despite the hollers of rejection, we will speak freely sharing the word of God openly, whether it is accepted or not as the word tells us to. We are called to preach the word, being prepared in season and out of season, correcting, rebuking, and encouraging with outstanding patience and careful instruction. So, listen and hear what the Spirit of the Lord is saying through me, take heed and repent for the time has come for the Kingdom to be established on earth as it is in Heaven.

President Trump declared that his administration would be leading by example on the liberty of religion in the United States, as he stated and I quote, "We are giving our churches their voices back." In the Rose Garden at the National Day of Prayer event

President Trump said, "Faith is deeply embedded into the history of our country, the spirit of our founding and the soul of our nation." "We will not allow people of faith to be targeted, bullied or silenced anymore."

To this I say, THANK YOU Mr. President Trump!!! Discrimination against spiritual beliefs restrains and oppresses the people of God. But Christ came to set the oppressed free, and His spirit is upon us. As the church, the spirit of God lives within our temples, and the word that lives within us is Life.

As Galatians tells us, we are called to be free, as brothers and sisters in Christ we use our freedom to serve one another humbly in love.

The law is fulfilled completely by loving each other as we love ourselves, so as we freely share our beliefs, we share the love of God that is within each of us.   The move of our love is a powerful force of transformation, and our love eradicates evil and changes the face of our world into a glorious paradise.   We have been given the authority to cast out demons, to drive away unclean spirits, and to heal every kind of disease and sickness.   There is a health crisis in this world, because the church has been silent.   The power of the people is greater than policies, not only do we conquer all impossibilities; we have all the power over the enemy.

The Second, this administration is working to bring the bible back into the classrooms of America, and this is something to seriously rejoice about. Our children need to know the truth, and the bible is our only good news. We are to train up our children in the way that they should go, and once the word takes root in their hearts, in old age it will not depart. Jesus said, let the children come to Him and hinder them not, so this here along is an amazing start. We have had attacks on our schools in this Nation, and under attack we must pray. The devil is after children, so we cover them under Jesus Christ's Blood. Let nothing come against the will of God, it is up to us to teach the young. This is major, gun control is one thing, but the word of God is Greater. Let no weapon come against us, but if it does may God protect us.

Even better, in the movement of Christ's spirit, setting prisoners free is also biblical. Bringing forth the proclamation of Isaiah 61, as Jesus said the Spirit of the Lord is upon me. The Lord has anointed us to preach good tidings to the poor, He has sent us to heal the brokenhearted, and to proclaim Liberty to the captives, and to open the prisons for those who are locked up. This is the acceptable year of the Lord, and the Day of God's vengeance is upon us. Slowly but surely, we are doing what He called us to do, even what the enemy does will turnout for good. Let us comfort those who mourn, and give them beauty for their ashes, and joy flowing as oil. We will be called the trees of Righteousness, planted by God and glorified.

Rebuilding the old ruins, raising up former desolations. Repairing the ruined cities, the destructions of many generations. Strangers shall stand together with us and feed the flocks. The sons of foreigners will plow and dress the Gardens. We are named the priests of the Lord, and we will come together to serve Our God. Eating the riches of the Gentiles, while boasting in their glory. Instead of shame we shall have double honor, instead of confusion rejoicing.

And finally, is the legalization of hemp which brings us one step closer to creating the New World of the Future. Hemp is one of the best natural resources there is, using hemp to its full potential can help save this world. Food, clothing, toiletries, health products, gasoline, structures and more, the benefits of hemp are galore. This is a good thing, and a step in the right direction, just hemp butter along can solve world hunger problems. I know there might be some conservatives starting to worry, but all herb is good, it is written in the bible. God gave us this world, and all its natural resources, we must use everything correctly according to His purpose. If we made our vehicles hemp compatible, forget exhaust problems, it will help our environment. Just imagine structures made stronger than steel, hemp has that ability, and we will build and build. Building up the Kingdom of Heaven, it only makes sense to build every family a mansion. Jesus said it and I believe, the same Spirit He has lives in you and me. In preparing a place for us, we become the open vessels for God to use our hands for His Mighty Works. The Kingdom is in Our Hands, and we will do greater things than Christ has done. It is Written. Amen.

Now, we have the promise of sharing dreams and creating the visions of the future which are possible through agreements and trust. Know that as we release our dreams kept hidden, the horizons will open the blessings of fulfillment.

Coming out of the dark corners as the light filling a room, we speak only the truth in love. It is a few days after mid-term elections and the news is full of dramatic events. On this day of November 9, 2018, the headlines are heart-breaking and infuriating. We grieve another tragic mass shooting, Paradise is on fire, election recounts are in demand, and our President is banning reporters and insulting Kellyanne Conway's husband. The articles about the survivors are few in comparisons to the articles about Trump, and I am disheartened.

I want us as a Nation of God to take some time and reflect on the things that truly matter, and that is our lives. No one knows the day or the hour of when our time is to come, and we are called home. Yes, there is a caravan of immigrants hoping to arrive in America from the South, and our troops have orders to fire upon thrown rocks. But where is the humanity?

I watched the video that showed the brokenness of a man when he was asked what he would do if he met President Trump, and he said that he would cry because that is all he can do. We who know the word understand that those who sow with tears will reap with songs of joy. The weepers are blessed with laughter, and God wipes away every tear from our eyes. We are to be compassionate and never cruel, denying asylum to immigrants before a trial and fear propaganda is unemphatic.

Yesterday while registering a patient for chemotherapy, the news announced the Thousand Oaks mass shooting. The elderly weak Caucasian woman looked me in the eyes, and with disgust said, "I know it's the people from the caravan, and we need to just shoot them at the border as soon as we see them." She obviously bought into the fear from this administration and believes there is an invasion coming. She later found out it was not an illegal immigrant that killed innocent Americans, but an ex-marine. President Trump says there is an invasion, because he says there is an invasion. However, the caravan is still weeks away and the temperature is steadily dropping to almost impossible travel. We should not kill people who want help, and we know that much responsibility comes with being blessed. Those who lend to the needy lend to God, let us not ever forget that. Our president campaigned on building a wall with Mexico's money, and now there is 5,000 people tracking to our country looking for work. I believe in building bridges and not walls, but still we are able to help them as well as our fellow American's in need. We need homes for the homeless, and food for the hungry, and it can be done quickly and beautifully the right way.

The book of Isaiah tells us that foreigners will pasture flocks, build houses, and plant vineyards. We are called to show our love to the strangers and alienated, because we once were aliens in the land of Egypt. We are all foreigners in a strange land, and this earth is not our home. We are only going through a test, and since the class is failing, here comes the curve. We are to love our neighbors as ourselves despite our differences and treat everybody the same way that we want to be treated. We do not walk in fear, but with power and soundness. Read Matthew 25:35 and see the spirit of Christ that is in us in all people, Jesus said that He was that stranger in need of food and drink that we let in. To have a good reputation in Heaven we must do what pleases God over pleasing man. In showing hospitality to strangers and helping those in distress, we never know if we could be entertaining angels. Have you not read that the Lord watches over the sojourners and the poor? It is wicked to devise plans of evil against those seeking refuge, and we are warned not to push them aside. We have all said Amen to the curse that comes to anyone that pervert's justice that is due to the foreigner.

If we want law and order then we must obey the whole law fully, and that simply means to love our neighbor as ourselves. 1 Corinthians 14:21 In the Law it is written, "By people of strange tongues and by the lips of foreigners will I speak to this people, and even then, they will not listen to me, says the Lord." If you won't listen to God, then what are the chances that you hear me? Let your spiritual ears open and accept His will for all of us. There is one body and one Spirit, and we all have our hope in one faith. We have no partiality and do not distinguish between the rich and the poor. Why do we value citizenship in the earth when our true citizenship is in Heaven? We should not live as though we want to stay here, we live as though we are leaving soon with our Savior.

There are rules to this life and breaking those rules have losing consequences. We are victorious and mighty overcomers in Christ Jesus. For Jeremiah told us, "For if you truly amend your ways and your deeds, if you truly execute justice one with another, if you do not oppress the foreigner, the fatherless, or the widow, or shed innocent blood in this place, and if you do not go after other gods to your own harm, then I will let you dwell in this place, in the land that I gave of old to your fathers forever." Jeremiah 7:5-7 And, in the end this is what it is truly about, we are all standing in blessings of our father Abraham. Every nation will flock to the Promise Land, and God has called us to be here together for His purpose. He asked us to gather and wait on Him, and He said that He will rise, and we will see His glory. It is the will of God for all of us to come together, and the opposition against this is the will of man.

Too many times blame is thrown out on both sides, and the middle ground is knowing the true side to be on. There are not good and bad people on both sides, the line of division must be drawn in the sand. We hear that democrats are wrong on these issues and republicans are wrong about others, but the truth is that we are not wrestling against people. The only one to blame in every dilemma we face is the enemy, and this enemy is not a person but a spiritual wickedness in High places. We do not wrestle against flesh and blood, but against principalities, powers, and rulers of darkness of this age, against spiritual wickedness in Heavenly places. These attacks are meant to breakdown our securities, and to overcome we must be prepared and vigilant. It is not the time to deny Christ in our state of union, because the government will rest on His shoulder. And, those who deny Jesus before men, will be denied before God in Heaven. These are the last days, and we live as though this is our only day promised. We know better than to worry about tomorrow, for each day is full of its own troubles.

We come together as One people and denounce the titles of separation that linger as trap of division. As we seek the Kingdom of God and righteousness above everything else, all our needs will be met. Whatever party of affiliation we belong to has no merit in the Kingdom that is to come. We are living our lives unto the Lord, and not to glorify man. His thoughts are far above our own, and to those of us who please Him, we will receive wisdom, knowledge, and happiness. We have seen man fall by doing what pleased him, but we will never fail by doing the will of God. Realizing that we need God's spirit over our own might releases the power in us through

Christ   to   do   all   things.

Remembering that without love we are nothing, and the act of charity is the greatest way to show the love within us. We who give to the poor lend to the Lord, and our reward is held in His Hands. The hidden treasures of knowledge and wisdom within us contain the mystery of Christ, and once opened our hearts are encouraged with unified love. Coming into full riches of pure blessings, the peace that surpasses all understanding engulfs our passions. We love others as we are loved in action and in truth. We are not embarrassed by our faith, and we do not straddle the fence to fit in with the ways of the world contrite to Christ. We know that the things that are impossible with people are possible with God. As we receive our new heart and spirit, we are cleansed from all unrighteousness.

Be not deceived by the powers that be but empowered to be the people that overcome all obstacles that have been. We the people of the United States can light up this dark world, when we come together as one force of reckoning. United in Christ, we rest the state of our being on His shoulders.

May our hearts be encouraged, knitted together in love, reaching all the riches of full assurance in the understanding and knowledge of God's mystery, which is Christ. We are His workmanship, created in

Christ Jesus for good works, which God prepared ahead of time, so we would walk in them. We know that God causes all things to work together for good to those who love God, to those of us who are called according to His purpose. We did not choose God, but He chose us, and appointed us to go out and bear fruit, so that our fruit remains, and whatever we ask of Our Father in Jesus Name, it will be given to us. Obtaining an inheritance, predestined according to His purpose who is working out all things after the will of His counsel.

The Lord is with us, He is at Our Head, and His priests with their battle trumpets to sound the call to battle against us.

As the Children of Israel, we do not resist, because we know that no one succeeds by fighting against the God of our fathers. The Trumpets blow at the new moon, the full moon and on the day of our feast. The eagle cries out with a loud voice as it flies over our heads, three wailing woes to those of us dwelling on the earth, blasting the trumpets the Angels are all three blowing. Do not hold back the tears and the sobs, cry aloud, lifting up the voices of Zion like a trumpet, declare to God's people their transgressions, the house of Jacob is called to repentance for their sins. Gathering the elect from the four winds, from one end of the heavens to the other, the Angels make the call with the Sounding of a loud trumpet, hear and recognize the summons. The Great and Dreadful Day is upon us, the trumpets will blow, and all who were lost and driven out will come to worship the Lord Our God on the Holy Mountain at Jerusalem. Sound the alarm on the Holy Mountain, blow the trumpet in Zion, let all the inhabitants of earth tremble in fear, for the day of the Lord is Coming, it is HERE!

Descending from heaven with a cry of command, the voice of an archangel, as the Sound of God's trumpet, the Dead in Christ Arise! In a moment, every eye will twinkle, at the last trumpet's sounding we shall all be changed, born-again raised in the Body of Christ as imperishable. As the seventh angel blows his trumpet, voices in heaven declare, "The kingdom of the world has become the kingdom of our Lord and of his Christ, and he shall reign forever and ever." The nations raged, but the wrath of God came, and the time for the dead to be judged, and for the rewarding of the servants, the prophets and the saints, and those who fear the name of the Lord, both small and great, and for the destroying the destroyers of this world. The Lord appears over us, and His arrow goes forth like lightening; the Lord Our God sounds the trumpet and marches forth in the whirlwinds of the south. The second woe has passed, and the third woe is soon to come. Blessed and Holy are we who share in the first resurrection! Over such the second death has no power, but we are called priests of God and of Christ, and we will reign with Christ Jesus for a thousand years. Amen.

The Lord is king over all of the earth, and we are one in Him, as He is the One over us. The mystery is that we will not all sleep but awaken, and we will be transformed into His image, at the last trumpet. When the signal is raised on the mountains, we look! And, when the trumpet is blown, we hear!

Chapter 2

Letter to President Donald Trump

My question to our president…

@realDonaldTrump President Donald Trump, would you please consider bringing both parties together, by having Democrats and Republicans partner up for a week, sitting by each other and eating lunch together? It would be God's will if forgiveness and friendship happened!

My letter written to President Donald Trump

January 11, 2019

Dear President Trump,

Building a wall is not the solution, but a barrier. Blocking out those who seek refuge is not a defense, but it is an offense to God. A house divided cannot stand in judgment, and we are urged to turn away from those who disagree and hinder the body of believers. We must come together on one accord and agree, so that there is no divide among us. Having the same mind, knowing right from wrong; we the people fight for the good cause of this whole world.

Concentrating on what really matters, we work together to make this world great. We bring life giving resources that enhance our everyday lives for the better, overcoming the impossible by conforming our minds to the law.

We do not serve ourselves, but we serve the people. Internecine oppression of party slandering, and casting blame on the Democrats or Republicans instead of sitting at the table together to agree is a method of destruction. Hear this! The solution is already written, and it is pleasing to the ears of man who hear and see the promises. As the Beckon of hope, the Light of the whole world who sits out on a pillar, we are not kept hidden, but shine as a reliable source of provision, supporting the needs of all people. Political policies and promises should come hand in hand with serving the needs of the people.

We have widows and orphans, the homeless and the imprisoned that need of reformation. The sick and the mentally perplexed that need a healing health system that works. Today, January 11, 2019, in the infusion clinic I work at, three cancer patients on a money-making Medicare supplement plan have been denied coverage for their ongoing treatment to save their life. There are many more that are being oppressed by a government that is working to boost the ego of man, claiming to be the party of values but have shown immoralities and corruptness at high levels. Also, on today, thousands go without the funds they have worked for, and most Americans are only a paycheck or two away from being thrown out on the streets. This is our reality, and as the smoke is settling, we see clearly that we are worried about the wrong thing.

A wall is just obstructing the justice that needs to prevail from a corrupt government that is headed to hell. We must repent, and turn around, concentrate on the truth, and rebuke the lies. Walls tumble down and fall, ask the people of Jericho. By faith the walls of Jericho fell, after the army had marched around them for seven days. The trumpets sounded, and at that sound the men gave a loud shout, and the walls collapsed. So, everyone charged straight in, and they took the city. A wall will not fix our border situation; history tells us that even if the gates are securely barred with no one coming in or out, the Lord can deliver His land on command to whomever He chooses.

God showed Ezekiel the entrance of the court, and when he looked there was a hole in the wall. Great shame and trouble came when the gates of Jerusalem were broken, and its walls were destroyed by fire. Gates open, and walls fall, but the time will come when we will extend our boundaries and build walls. After seeking God and with Him on our side, we will build up our territory and prosper. The

Lord says that He will be a wall of fire, and His glory will be a resting place for a multitude of men. If there be a wall, let it be of division between the holy and the profane.

Jeremiah warned us, that God tears down the walls of those who have sinned, and His vengeance is an unwelcomed avoidable fate. The oppressed, the sojourner, the least of mankind are the called and chosen people of God. Let us reason together, and compromise so that we are all satisfied with the end result. Those who come running to better their circumstance are not the enemy, but those who do harm and oppress are evil.

We are the Repairers of the breach, the people to restore law and order to the streets where we live. We are called to rebuild the ancient ruined cities forgotten and rise up the age-old foundations that lay desolate and barren. We have the manpower to build new houses for every family, and to plant gardens in each yard. Let us do the work that we are called to do and recreate the lost civilizations of Ancient Days.

So no, I am not saying to open all borders and let everyone in, but let us rebuild lost abandoned cities, plant gardens and build highways in the desert, clear the way for the Lord in the wilderness, and hear the voice that is calling us to unification.

We should organize every man that needs to work and go out to the places that are dark and shine our Lights all around. Let us research and find the ruined cities to bring them back to life, recreating them as they were before to be a place of refuge for the foreigner.

We have many places all over this world to clean up and restore, and I will list a few below for pondering. Mesa Verde, in Colorado thrived with ancient Anasazi people, and there are houses that have as many as 150 rooms. The great Mayan cities of Mexico, Belize, Guatemala, and Honduras laid ruined are ready to be beautified and inhabited again, Calakmul and Tikal are two of the largest Mayan cities, and they were powerful and great long ago and will be again. The overgrown forest in Palenque needs cultivation, and the crops planted will be plentiful.

We have the lost Aztec villages which were once a place of pilgrimage like Teotihuacan. There is Pompeii; Memphis in Egypt, the lost city of Machu Picchi, Palmyra, Ciudad Perdida, Carthage and it goes on and on. All over the earth, there are abandoned cities and ghosted towns that are waiting for the breath of life's restoration. This is what we must do; we will reach our hands out to our neighbors and help them restore their forgotten land. This will benefit all of us, and we will come together in love and do the work needed without complaining or grumbling. We will rejoice together at harvest time and live peacefully in the earth as good stewards. God bless America and this whole world, with His favor and provisions.

All things are possible, and the word will be fulfilled before the coming of Christ.

The wealth of the wicked is held up for the Righteous, and I beseech you President Trump to seek the Kingdom of God first, turn from all wickedness, and use all of your wealth and resources for the poor. Become the example of a camel passing through the eye of a needle, and I pray that all the rich follow after you according to the will of God. And, this is how we will bring forth the Kingdom of Heaven on earth. President Donald Trump will pay for it, *smile*. Amen. God bless and keep you all until the coming of Christ.

Truthfully and with Love Always,

Tonisha Fortune

Chapter 3

Let this mind be in you

Coming together with the same mind, we bring forth ALL things New in due time. Knowing that love conquers all, we have the victory without fail. Having no division among us, we stand strong in correcting all wrongs.

Looking at this life as present day, we see darkness mixed with light, and evil amid good. Knowing that good always wins over evil in the end, and love conquers hate, the way is already made. If we call out our current administration and hold them accountable for their words from beginning to end, we are justified in speaking out against the hypocrisy and will not be silenced. The past is over, and this is the day that matters the most, so there is no point of referencing what has long been over, the leader in office now is in the hot seat, if it is too hot to handle, let him drop it. As our sitting president danced to the song singing that he did it his way, confirmation was revealed that the end of the world as we knew it was near.

Witnessing wickedness in high places, and the wealth of the wicked spilling over the walls and into the streets, we are not fighting the person but their principles. Those of us who care for people more than ourselves, are justified in standing against the authority of rulers who assert dark powers in our world.   United as troops in battle formation, we declare that the trumpets blow, and we are not intimidated by loud barks with no bite. The control and manipulation through forcefully silencing the oppressed, as a way to rise, will soon drop back a slap of reality in the face. Our words are powerful and will not be muted in the face of the deceitful. It is the truth and nothing but the truth, so help us God. There is but one liar fathering many through influence, let the truth set us all free and we will be free indeed.

We are to give and not take, turn away from violence and not attack, and take care of our poor instead of taking from them. Those who do not want to feed, shelter, clothe, and give medical attention to the needy are counted among the damned due to being selfish and greedy. The eye of the needle will not grow wider for the camel to pass through, but if he becomes small in his mind through humility then he may pass through.

What has changed regarding this nation's morality, in the US of A over the last 50 years, was the sanctity defiled over time as more and more people turned from God?

Why such a falling away from the days of the Apostolic to reformation diluted?

If a child can learn common core knowledge, why the resistance of teaching the golden rule?

As slaves were denied the right to know the truth as a method to keep them ignorant of their power, our children are being hindered while facing a generation of people who do not love. If our children are taught to believe in Santa, the Easter Bunny, the tooth-fairy, and even a frightening elf on a shelf, what more harm can be done by letting them embrace Jesus? LET THE CHILDREN COME!!

*2 Timothy 3:1-5 ....'This know also, that **in the last days** perilous times shall come. For men shall be lovers of their own selves, covetous, boasters, proud, blasphemers, disobedient to parents, unthankful, unholy, without natural affection, trucebreakers, false accusers, incontinent, fierce, despisers of those that are good, traitors, heady, high-minded, lovers of pleasures more than lovers of God; Having a* *form of godliness, but denying the power thereof: from such turn away.*

Some study the bible for instruction, others look for their own ways of living-good and bad intentions, others are stuck in the no way out mentality. Whatever path we go down we all end up in the same place at the end, and there is joy in hoping that once we get there, we will be made right. Whether you believe that it is possible to love with or without God, or to feel empathy for the least at your greatest, the actions of each individual speaks after thought. This last year reads out like the end time prophecies of the bible, the division in the house predicts a falling of great demise, rumors of wars, earthquakes, natural disasters bring about the labor pains of birthing out a New Nation of world order.

Distractions, discouragement, and deflections are tactics of the suppressor, and we abhor those traits in our leadership, and rebel against dictatorship as bureaucratic states of people. The perfection of unification is forming, and the way to get there is not by the strength of one, but all. Having the ability to comprehend and interpret our constitutional rights, we bring about tranquility. Though President Trump claimed in the past that he is the only one that can save us, and only he can make America great again, we claim false. Let that be added to the pot of lies and controversy stirred, for there is only one Savior and He does not come for just America but for this whole world, and if we humble ourselves and pray, seeking the face of God and repent, then God will listen to us, forgive us, and heal our land.

Let us not boast about how great we are, but our weakness is worth talking about, for His strength is made perfect in us when we are weak. Let us instead boast on others and uplift and edify each other constantly.

With these being the times of seducing spirits let our faith unite as one, having no cares for this life or deceitfulness of wealth, we eat the fruits of the word without choking. Our eyes are open, and we turn away from the dark into the Light, from evil to good. Looking for our inheritance in sanctified bodies marked with the blood of forgiveness, receiving all promises from the Kingdom. The poor are welcomed and fed, the widows and fatherless are comforted, the captive and imprisoned set-free, and every need and desire in His will be fulfilled. We do not walk with the wicked, or go in the ways of sinners, and do not condone mockers. Our delight is in the Lord, and we meditate day and night on His law and do not depart from it.

Our President complained on Christmas that he was all alone as he angrily tweeted, but the government shutdown will not keep meat from his table. Even though he promised us that he would not tweet after becoming President, this too is counted in the spiral of lies bringing down this administration. Meanwhile, Putin shared that he is ready to launch a new hypersonic nuclear missile; it is time to pay attention and disregard the distractions. Our priorities must be straight, and the whistle is blowing. Some parents just buried their children, and many of us have trouble enjoying the holidays due to lost love ones. There is a disconnection to the spirit of truth, and I pray that words shared in this book live and take root. There is a reason behind the season, and we must take the time to reflect and love other people.

We lift up the names of the children that have died at the hands of their parents, who tried to bring them over to the land of the free through unlawful passage. The innocent spirits of Felipe Gomez Alonzo and Jakelin Caal rest in the Hands of the Lord, and we embrace the words of Christ saying let the children come and hinder them not! Such as these are the Kingdom of Heaven and once we all trust in God as children do, we will see the Kingdom. As health checks are called for and healing is restored, may we all taste and see the goodness of the Lord. Be careful who we allow to speak into the minds of our children, because to question faith and belief is of demons.

We heard our President on the Christmas call, and saying to a seven-year-old who still believed in Santa Claus, that it is marginal is wild. I know that her innocence did not allow her to be phased, she is protected and covered by His grace. Instead of admitting being wrong and repenting Mike Huckabee defends with a line from the film, Fatal Attraction. Are you kidding? No, he did not boil a bunny, but his words are inappropriate and that's not ever funny. The news on Trump never ends, and just like Jesus said about Him the world could not hold all the books kept hidden, and for Trump this is true, if everything is written this book would never end.

On today, 12/26/2018 the reports read that the daughters of Trump's podiatrist exposed there were no bone spurs; it was just a favor between fathers to help our President evade going to war. No one is surprised by the avoided draft; that we already knew. As the stories keep coming, it's more that we can't believe. Tickled by the line of, "Believe me," know that we have been deceived. This craziness cannot be made up, it's like we fallen into the Twilight Zone and can't get up. As the word of truth is girdled around our loins, we know that the righteous fall seven times and rise again. But the wicked stumble and fall down into evil when calamity strikes.

Trump says that he is a nationalist, and that is good for that particular type of person benefiting the nation and political parties in America. Jesus says that He is the way, the truth, and the life, and we know that no one can get to God without Christ. Trump says that it is a very scary time for young men, but the word tells us that we do not have the spirit of fear but of power and a sound mind.

Trump says that he is proud to shut down the government, but we know that we are not to look after just our own interests but also the interest of others. Those of us who love the Lord take care of His sheep, and we will not leave them to be slaughtered by the wolves. We obey His teachings binding His words in the tablet of our hearts, and we will do all that He says to do.

This Christmas poem I wrote this year pretty much sums it up…

As life is but a dream; when it ends, we awake to the real scene. A dream within a dream; sleeping as the dead until awakening, dreaming.

You see, we live and die and live again in reverse, as the living were asleep until He rose.

Now, the curse is no more, and we rise knowing that all flesh is dead inside, and the spirit soars.

The body is just a vessel for our souls to ride,

and death is only another conquered fate

that's tried.

Delivered from birth our souls came down to

earth as intelligent life formed from the

Heavens above, developed in the world we

became trapped by the thoughts from below.

Knowing that we are aware of where we are

going when we leave this place; we have no

need to hold on to misconception.

Before being conceived in the womb, we

were set apart, known, and destined for

greatness.

WAKE UP! Stop dreaming and see. Oh now,

we are directing our own movie...

As we skip on to the End, we all know the

happy ending. Red, brown, yellow, black,

and white, we are all the same in His sight.

Do not doubt that we will all come together

as one, giving our differences to Jesus Christ,

the Son.

There's no argument to justify hate, and our

outside appearances and opinions fade away.

Nothing is impossible; all things can be done

when we realize our power.

Greater is He that is in us, than he that is in

the world. We are not from here, just sent to shake things up.

The earth is void and with no form, until the voice of God speaks and stirs the waters. Let it be known, our bodies do not matter, only the soul which lives forever.

Always love, and speak with grace, remembering forever that we are from a better place.

We come to shine Light from above, align our minds in Christ, and to do His will in love.

The Kingdom is in our hands, remove the

blinders, and may eyes twinkle.

Assorted CHRISTmas lights of ALL colors!

Be Merry and Love.

It is quite simple when we look at ourselves as the people who are called and Chosen to reign with Christ. Connected Lights of Love, spreading a glorious illumination of love across this world as a beckon of hope, we unite as Saints changing and claiming everything in our paths. Are we a nation of the people and by the people, or are we a nation of politics ran by parties? It was never supposed to be this way; we were called to live an abundant life of love, joy, and peace. Establishing a government founded on truth and law for the people and by the people, forsaking politics for the welfare of the governed. Yet, here we go. We see the rich take more and more, and the oppression of the poor is continually enforced. The government shutdown has no effect on the wealthy; they can go without a check or two without being evicted. But those who work to provide and pay for their own healthcare are faced with many perplexing out of their control situations. How to pay for food, childcare, and housing is a topic of disagreements that the word fixes with one sentence from Jesus, "Meet the needs of my Children".

As we sit low and look high, we ask for mercy and grace, so that the Lord will turn His face back to us. Having imaginations of the grand, we make the elections to come favorably changed by our hands.

Chapter 4

Reversing the curse with blessings

As I look at my country, the United States of America, my heart is burning with words of fire and passion that cannot be contained. Coming from a place of love and concern, I offer my perspective as a voice of truth unheard. After living almost forty years, and knowing the history of where I came from, I am blessed to have been born in a free country that allows me to have my own personal faith. Even more so, the gift of being able to share my beliefs is a blessing that I am grateful for. My background and experiences in life shape my views, and the reasoning behind my convictions is embedded deep in the roots of my soul. I am concerned for our country and the values that we have as a nation, for there is a lack of understanding. As I reflect and write, I pray that my personal feelings sink as a rippling rock in the waters, and that the spirit of truth flows out as a river. We know our past as Americans, and every one of us has a different background and opinion on the subject. Please, hear me out.

Fortunately, I was blessed to have my great-grandmother until she died at 101 years old when I was 18, and also my grandparents who shaped my thoughts from a child until now. When I think of how my great-great grandmother came to this country as a newborn baby from Africa, ripped away from her parents, and sold to my great-great-great grandfather, I imagine the pain her parents must have felt. To know that she was mistreated her whole life as a slave from birth until the grave; having seven black children for her husband and being raped by her master in order for my life to exist is surreal. For my great-grandfather Artemon to be taken from her and raised with his white siblings due to his light complexion had to have been hard for the master's wife to process. My great-grandfather made tombstones as a trade and worked closely with his brothers on both sides of the family. His white brothers often apologized for what their father did to his mother, and his black brothers had a friend on the inside of the plantation to make their burdens easier.

When the time came for him to marry, he chose a Creole girl named Amaya, and in their union, they raised a family of nine children, the youngest was my grandmother Jessie. My grandmother told me that her parents did not read or write, but they taught her a faith centering on forgiveness. She only went to school until 7th grade, because young black girls were being raped by white men on the several mile walk to school. Coming from a family that only spoke French; they were ridiculed and labeled as stupid for not speaking good English. She learned how to read and write after marrying my grandfather in the 50's, but due to embarrassment she never taught her children her native tongue.

My grandfather was a black man born to free

parents who were educators, and he outscored

many white men on a test that placed him as

the only black man in the engineering

department until his retirement. He told us

stories of how he had to carry the utility poles

on his back by himself as his white co-workers

taunted him, because they were jealous that he

passed the test and was able to tell them were

to put the poles. He also told me about their

change of heart, and how they defended him

when he was denied service in a restaurant due

to his skin color after work one evening. My

grandfather was a survivor of the Korean War,

and he came back home to America knowing

that he deserved better than the treatment he received as a veteran.

My mother was the third child of five, and she raised me as a single mother. I watched her struggle to pay the bills even though she worked two, and sometimes three jobs while going to school, and I had a diverse upbringing being educated in both "black" and "white" schools. I remember when we use to pray in school before the pledge of allegiance, and how we sang hymns of praises before class in the 80's. Looking at our country now I see the falling away as words of prophecy written.

I gave this information as a buffering before expelling my personal beliefs on current matters which are controversial to those who come from differing backgrounds than me. Each of our experiences shape who we are, and individual circumstances affect our views in life's current events. What matters to me might not be of importance to the next person, and vice versa. But, every one of us has a purpose that matters to the advancement of our world.

My voice speaks for the Kingdom, and my heart aches for this world. We are in this world, but not from here. We seek first the Kingdom, and then everything else after it will come. When I hear of people idolizing flags or shoes, I think on the things of Heaven and how this is not done in God's presence outside of this world. There will be no state or country flags planted on the grounds of Heaven and the robes of white that we will wear will have no emblem or name brand. There will be no division based on race, political affiliations, or religious denominations. We are one body of people with differences that work together to glorify the Kingdom, and in love we cover up all the wrongs of the past. We are walking in the world as the Light being Children of God, and our outside appearance does not matter. Our clothes are outward coverings, and they are meant to be given away to those who are without. What is the point of burning shoes when there are people walking around on bare feet? What meaning does a flag have outside of this world?   As a piece of fabric blowing in the wind, is it more important than the naked that need covering? It's cloth, and if it's cold outside it would be more useful wrapped around us as a blanket than on a pole in a stadium.

To sing an anthem with lyrics of pride for a nation divided only rings of hypocrisy when the love of people is not found in the hearts of man. Pledging allegiance to a Nation that claims to be one under God while forsaking the word has no nobility; our allegiance is to God and not man or

anything man-made. To be American means that we have the freedom to be individuals and we do not conform to the ways of this world. Those who love this world and the things in it do not love God. We do not look for acceptance from man, but to be accepted in the Kingdom. We have the right to speak what is on our minds and in our hearts, and we can choose not to participate in the everyday norms of society.

This is what makes America great, and to take away these simple freedoms is un-American. For many generations of my family America has yet to be great, but the Lord has given us a way of escape. Putting aside race, gender, religion, political and social status, we look at the hearts of our fellow Americans and greet each other in love with a holy kiss. The more we give love the less we will see hate, and once we all come together in Christ this world will be a better place. We are to love each other as Christ loved the Church, and since we are the church, we freely love others as we love ourselves.

As the Light, we stand out on the hill beckoning our voices on one accord guiding the lost. Hear these words in love and walk in the spirit and in truth always. Knowing what truly matters in the eyes of God, we have no worries about the thoughts of man. Having power and a sound mind, we know that the greatness in us overcomes this world. We release the blessings of Heaven on the earth, and we bind up every curse in this world. We stand up against the enemy who hates; resisting evil so that it will flee in the sight of our love. As we see each other for who we truly are, we accept our differences as a union of agreement. In love we overlook a multitude of faults, and perfect love casts away all fears and doubt. Coming together as one we are shielded from the storms of life under the umbrella of Christ. May we abide under His Shelter, and rest in the shadow of the Almighty God Always and Forever. I leave you with the peace and love of Christ until the coming of the Kingdom.

God bless you.

Prayers and love

Even though we disagree on somethings, I lift President Trump up to Our Father God in prayer. May the Lord work out His perfect salvation in him as He will all of us. Let him be slow to anger and quick to love. And, as

our leader I pray that he covers himself in

prayer and walk in God's grace from above.

As he learns patience, and watches his words,

may he seek knowledge and be wise in all

that he does. Keeping in mind the teachings

of Christ, we pray for unification and peace

and rebuke all division and strife.

Have your way Lord in our nation, let

your will be done, and all people accept

salvation.

In Jesus name we pray.

Amen.

We are as the people of Nineveh living in a great nation, the Lord has spoken out against us due to the aroma of wickedness brewing that has Him nauseated. The word speaks against the City of Babylon with woes of bitterness, but a hope remains in the sight of the faithful.

As Jonah did, many of us run away from the calling. However, there is no escape from what has been destined before the formation of this world. We have heard of the destruction, and the revelation to come. The Lord has given us a way of escape from His wrath, and it is available as long as the Lord can be found. We are the ones that run from the Lord, but we can't run from ourselves. Eventually we will bump into something and have no choice but to turn around and accept it. The Lord is in our hearts, and we cannot live outside of His beat.

The fear of being thrown out and not accepted ruffles us as the sea during a storm but running away does nothing but makes it rougher and causes alarm. As Jonah told the sailors, we will also be picked up and thrown into the treacherous sea, and the waters will not overcome us after the calm comes. As we are swallowed up whole but not eaten up, we sit in the darkness of our sins in full repentance.

Three days and three nights of constant prayer being distressed, depressed, and full of regrets, asking for help with tears pouring from the spirit. As the dead live in Christ, so are we as Jonah given another chance at life. Knowing always that salvation comes from God alone, no man can save us. As vomit coming from the mouth like spoilage from being left out, we are spit out into the world of man. Having a second chance, the Lord repeats His command to us to share the message given. We obey and go without defiance because we have learned through chastisement.

The Lord had decided to overthrow the city and destroy it, just as He says He will do to the Great Nation of Babylon. However, He changed His mind simply because the people believed Him. He turned His anger away and gave compassion in its place. And, the same grace is available to us if we humble ourselves and pray, seek His face and turn from our wicked ways.

The Lord who has given us a glimpse of the future has done so not to scare us, but to prepare us. As we say, "Yes Lord we believe in you and on you and stand on your word." His wrath softens, and He gives us His Kingdom in pleasure instead of destruction.

As the people of Nineveh did, so must we do. Let us proclaim a fast, calling urgently on God, giving up our evil ways and all acts of violence. God has shown us that He can turn fierce anger into the compassion needed to keep us from perishing.

At this news we should rejoice, unlike Jonah who became depressed to the point of suicidal thoughts. He knew God's compassion, temperament, and love so he was ready to leave the earth. With it not being His time, the Lord gave him shelter and shade to cover his pain. As the plant died the Lord reminds us that we must tend to the things He gives us to make it grow. Just as it grew in one night, it died the next. We have been taught to have more concern over people than plants, and when the Lord tells us to go, we will obey.

Just as Jonah sat in the belly 3 days and nights, Christ Jesus went to the devil's den and got the keys for our sakes. We have been given the signs and have no need to wonder about the miracles to come. For we believe in the words of our Savior and know that greater is He that lives in us. And we shall do greater than what Christ did.

Whatever we bind on the earth will be binded in Heaven, and what we lose in the earth will be loosed in heaven. We ask for our Father to turn His face to us, and to give us His Kingdom as promised. It is already here, and it is seen with eyes of the spirit, as every eye twinkle and the change removes the blinders, we will see the fullness thereof in all of His glory in the earth. Believe this! Amen.

It is not the will of God for His Children to perish, for He has asked us to take care of His Flock, feeding His Sheep and cherish. We have all power in our Hands and being in His image we will do ALL that He commands.

As One people in the Body of Christ, we walk in compassion and speak life.

Greater is He that is in us, than He who is in the world. We who are His Children are gods, did you not know this? He has made us to do His will in the earth, we are called Saints, and we have the authority to judge and change this world.

Jesus answered them, Is it not written in your law, I said, Ye are gods? John 10:34

Do ye not know that the saints shall judge the world? and if the world shall be judged by you, are ye unworthy to judge the smallest matters? 1 Corinthians 6:2

Some might see this world as separate countries, divided by language and beliefs. But, we are One earth and One people connected through soul ties invisible to the natural eye of looks and bonded by the spirit.

If we can see them, we can feed them.

Life and death is in the power of our tongue, and the Lord has given us the means to take care of everyone.

Hunger is not a God issue, but a lack of godly officials.

The Lord did not create us as robots, we are made in His image and have the power to create as He is the Creator.

Only God can change the heart of man, no one is lost beyond being found.

No man is greater than the next, without love we are nothing. The master is not greater than the servant, and the Children

of God are sent to serve. It is greater than

man versus woman and republicans against

democrats, it takes us all to come together as

One body in Christ to bring forth the

Kingdom.

The glory our eyes will see is the

Coming of the Lord, so we can overlook the

sight of dysfunction and wait on the reign of

the Holy One.

Prayer changes things.

I believe the word of God is true, and He said

that He is working out His salvation in us all.

I know it looks grim, but there is hope for us

even yet. We must pray.

There is good and evil in us all. It is time to come together and not separate, so we rise above and do not fall.

The Lord told us to pray for our appointed leaders, it is for our benefit as much as his.

What is meant for evil, the Lord turns it to good. The end is already written, the enemy does not win. We are wrestling spirits not people, and love covers a multitude of sins.

NO MORE SEPARATION OF THE CHURCH AND STATE FOR IT IS LIKE SEPARATING THE SOUL FROM THE BODY WITH THE SAME FATE.

You really think Obama is at fault?

Oh beforehand, America was great when it was accepted to hate people based on characteristics and not character. American never dealt with race relations before Obama, but only swept it under the rug. After a man of color won office, and cleaned house, the rug was shaken, and the dirtiness was shown to the world.

Being sober and alert we stand up to the adversary that roars as a lion walking around seeking to devour. Standing in faith knowing that all our afflictions are accomplished in Christ, we suffer for only a short while. Being made perfect through grace, called into eternal glory we are strengthen and settled in the ways of God. To God alone be the glory and dominion for ever and ever. Amen.

On Friday, December 7, 2018, I called into the Al Sharpton's Freedom Friday show to ask him how he felt about the political parties uniting in love, and I was disheartened to hear him say that it could not happen. After greeting him I said, "Knowing that we are a Chosen race, a royal priesthood, a holy nation, a people for His own possession, that we may proclaim the Excellencies of Him who called us out of darkness into His marvelous Light, how do you feel about uniting the political parties with love? Let us concentrate on what can be agreed upon according to the word and accepting our differences as strengths to build us up with positive words, because life and death are in the power of the tongue-our words live. I also asked him how he would feel about a new political party that unites us in Christ called the church, made up of all people. Or even challenging the rule of separation of church and state, because we are not of this world and we know that if we deny Christ, we will be denied the rights to the Kingdom to come. Al Sharpton told me that it could never happen, because there are people who will not change their minds on important issues. However, I know that nothing is impossible with God, and His will be done over our own.

There are no good and bad people on both sides, but we must separate good from evil. The ways of this world are not the ways of God! The church has a voice of unity on one accord, and it is time to come out of the prayer closet and proclaim the truth in the streets. We come to set all the captives free, the only law that matters is to love others as we love ourselves. We are servants of Christ not served by man but serving God through acts of charity. By faith, we do not look at the circumstances of this life but call out the things that are not in existence into reality. What is not possible for man is possible with God, and once we surrender our will over for His will, it will be done.

In searching for an artist to draw the cover for this book, I reached out to a few people I knew that could draw. One being Vic Kingrey, he laughed when I told him that I would change his name to Victory King if he refused to agree to this mention. He agreed. Being that he had many questions for me, I decided to share some of our messages in this book to help others understand the conveyance of this book.

Vic- Well my biggest burning question is who is your target audience?

Me- All people who believe, or not, those in need of the twinkling that removes the blinders.

Vic- Serious question. Do you love Donald Trump?

Me- I love all people and my enemies more so I guess you would need to read the book to understand me.

Vic- DO you love all white people? And the great white hope Donald J. Trump? I may not understand much but I know an answer that comes from deep down in a person's heart when I hear one.

Me-I don't see white people the way that you do...lol. everybody is black to me. Especially you and even Trump...lol. No such thing. We are all the same, even Chinese or black. Everybody. I can't hate people because they genes mutated. That's cruel. I love everybody the same and see no color. I might be coming off as sarcastic through messenger so please don't get offended, it's all love.

Vic- I won't assume things about you if you extend the same courtesy. My questions always seem a little loaded, but you will see that questions they are only. No nefarious intent. Well mostly And I couldn't agree more. Race is the most irrelevant characteristic there is.

Vic- How long have you been interested in the political machinations and shenanigans of our time?

Me- Yes. I have a weird mindset that some might not understand, so I write to explain my views. There's no race or denomination in Heaven and that's how we must live on earth.

I have been an internet political social guru since Myspace...2006. My first book back then scared some people away. So, I am tiptoeing back in...

Vic-I'm made of especially stout stuff. The only thing that scares me like a little girl are the wasps risen from hell Hornets etc. Demons. So, tell me how you see it all.

Me- I want to create a new party but I am running out of time for 2020...maybe 2024. My only supporters are from UK and India...but I need to promote it more.

Vic-I read that earlier today.

Me-Demons flee at the name of Jesus and He lives in me. No fear only Power and a sound mind.

Vic-If I may leave that wish of yours on the table for a short while longer, There is a ton of information I must understand along the path that leads us to this unique decision and conversation

Me-Take your time but I move with the spirit, once the book is ready the cover will be done. Thank you.

Vic-Compassion and love are the most trying and painful things a person can give to another. If done correctly agree or disagree?

Me-I agree. Serving others over self-serving.

Vic-Sometimes, every once in a while, we need our feelings hurt and our pride trampled. It is what, idk, reason numero uno neglected trait to teach others now.

Me-Amen. We all have our crosses to bear, and there is glory promised for the pain.

Vic- And a sense of worth. For a lot of members of all the various faiths in the world belief comes easy, motivation, etc... Humility is often the virtue that is so Damn out of reach. Can also be argued that if humility is not with you, it is then one of the biggest detriments to one's cause. Agree or disagree

Me-I agree. I study many faiths and religions for commonality. It's there, and when we stop focusing on the differences, we can see it. The Bible has Jesus who preached that the

Kingdom is in us and all are welcome, the Qur'an which agrees that the Kingdom is to be created by our hands, and the Sikhs who have the right idea with the temple for all people regardless of faith to worship and eat free at the Golden Temple. It's not about separating but coming together in love, this world is capable of becoming good everywhere. Love conquers hate.

Vic-Actions speak louder than words. Agree or disagree?

Me- Yes, I agree, and that is what I shared in my book, Seeking. We have to do the work to see the Kingdom, it does not come with observation but creation.

Vic- I'll slow down. With the silly quizzes by the way. Promise they weren't frivolous

Me-I don't mind, it's nice. You should ask questions before making any decisions. Dangerous people could come after us just for trying to unite races. It's crazy in the world, but we are not from here.

Vic-So, you think Trump is your enemy?

Me-No. We do not wrestle with people but spirits and wickedness in high places. The wealth of the wicked is held up for us, and we are coming to take it from the poor. It's deeper than that. The Anti-Christ spirits dwells in leadership connected to many dictators with like minds. I come with the truth with the only purpose of destroying the works of the enemy through the love of God. We have all been here before and this is the end, after the Last Days we reign. I have pictures to prove it ...

Me- I have Putin's photo and Trump's from back then...even sessions. And Buddha statue...you won't believe it but it's Kim Jong Un and we rub the belly. It's real, but that's another book. Lol

Pontius Pilates aka John Kelly

Caesar aka Putin

Vic- I have a Buddha statue

Me- I was joking on the last one by the way .

Vic- My roommate has a cat named Putin

Me- I believe we could conjure the wrong spirits through unholy vessels. Trump is a vessel that needs repentance as we all do, I plan to share the gospel in love. A Jesus overkill on this administration convicting both parties and coming to a resolution of one body- The Church.

Me-I speak the truth, tell no one. The Russians are watching us.

Vic- Everyone is watching us.

Me- I know. But, God. We win.

Me- This conversation is going in the book with your permission....of course. Or I change your name to Victory King.

Vic- Grants consent

Me- It's not about the book, it's way bigger than that. I will

cleverly write it in love with the grace of God.

Words live, and minds will change. Believe

that.

Chapter 5

Behind the times, Logging in to vote

Digital technologies have just as much of an effect on politics as outdated poll machines have in the voting process. Comparing the two considering our advancements as individuals since the invention of poll machines, we can see that our digital technology is far above our prehistoric political system. As we check facts in real time, read news updates around the clock, and see the skeletons in the closets of candidates on the social media outlets, we see more of who and what we are voting into office. With that being said, in hindsight considering our recent elections some might wonder what happened to America. Oh, the Great Beautiful has fallen into disgrace, and the people have turned away from our first love, God.

With digital technologies we are reaching more and more people, and those of like minds attract to each other. As we listen to the messages something resonates with each person based off of their personal insights to what is being said. We then decide whether or not we like the candidate or not, if there is a candidate that is unfavorable before considering the message, we then spread disdained messages to influence the masses. Those that hate divide and those that love, unite. We can easily see the prophecy of biblical pretense unfolding, when we read the scripture that says in the Last Days there will be a great falling away.

Back when there were no advanced technologies in politics, the Bible belt in America was wider. Politicians were known as liars and hardly trusted except for honest Abe, but their true integrity was not shown until after they took office. With our digital technologies, we have more of an insight into who the Politician is, based off of who they were in the past. Social media then kicks in and spreads this virus of negativity through every circuit of cyberspace until it has covered the majority. This is a good thing, even though the intent may be evil. If we look at the internet as a source of information whether it is good or bad, we find that the resourcefulness and convenience of technology has positively impacted our lives. If anything, it is a revelation of who people are and what they stand for.

If we want to make politics possible in a digitally technical world, our system has to meet the advancements of technology and function according to the needs of the people. We can examine impossibilities of digital technologies in politics, by observing people with social media outlets in their hands, viewed standing outside in line for hours waiting to vote on outdated machines in inclement weather. As we are a generation of now and fast since the invention of the microwave, could there be a more convenient, accurate, and efficient way to count everyone's vote?   Perhaps tablets like the doctor offices have...

Would it be too hard in our technical world to link the social security numbers of the deceased to voting offices in live time? We can use digital technologies to advance our political process into the New Age, based on utilizing the tools we already have available to its full potential. Due to digital technologies, we no longer have to wait for snail mail for we can email, we do not have to get out in the traffic to shop for our best buys because we can shop online, and we can find out information on people and things at a fingers touch instead of researching for hours at the library. So, what if we did not have to fill out paper cards to register to vote, or stand in lines to use prehistoric voting machines, and we used the technologies that are available to us digitally and registered and voted online?

After having the internet all of these years, we should have figured out a way to make this happen. Now, should we beat ourselves up for being behind the times? No. But, we should move forward in a timely manner and get busy catching up to where we need to be. Imagine if tablets were delivered to the hands of voters instead of ballots. We can format them to help the handicap, and to speak the instructions if need be. More people could vote at the same time, because it is easier to distribute than setting up a voting poll. The results would come in live time, and there will be no delay tallying votes.

Moving to a New World order is not an evil thought, but a good thing to embark on. The Church and State are separate, but the Lord has called the Church to be His governing Body of people over the state of man. We must not look at the ways of the old as stuck in the past; however, it is steps into the future. We are moving forward, and technology is the way to advance into the next political phase. Using our resources online, we can find and network with others who are willing to work to create the perfect union the preamble speaks of. We must come together as a people to change the political process. It is not the tools, the gadgets, or even technology itself that has the power to help or harm, but the people that are behind the screen with evil or good intentions that matter.

The spirit of a person exposes the intent behind the use of digital technologies, so digital technology does not influence. We have power over social media, we choose what to read, believe, and share. Once we take back our power as a people, and recognize who the true enemy is, we can strategize a plan to make all things possible. We can look at our world and see wonderfulness and wickedness; there is a spirit of Christ and the Anti-Christ. We are wrestling against spiritual wickedness in High Places.

Who speaks contradictions to the teachings of Christ, and brings with Him followers who portray themselves as sheep but underneath they are wolves in fake clothes? Jesus said to us, come all who are weary and rest, the opposer says go away to all of those who are in need. The Lord says give, the enemy says take. Jesus says provide food, water, shelter, clothes, heal the sick, and go to the prisoners, the adversary despises charity and wants to lock up everyone who offends him. Christ our Lord says love your neighbors as yourself, and He explained who our neighbor is-(the next country), the suppressor says, "Build a wall to keep the neighbors out!" God says love your enemies, and pray for those who persecute you, the devil says destroy them and their children. We, who are called Saints, let us decide for ourselves if it was the will of God or the will of man this past election.

As the Lord instructs, let us declare fasting and prayer, for we see the red states as fired destruction. Knowing it is written, prophesied and witnessed, we repent and humbly come before the world as Servants. Let the Church come forth and stand united as the umbrella of services needed to those who are called Sheep. From the orphaned to the widow, the sick and shut-in, those who are hungry, homeless, or helpless, the oppressed and the depressed, all of us who have been wounded, abandoned, or afflicted, feel the embrace of Christ's loving comfort of grace, peace, favor and abundant joy.

As He overcame the world, we are Overcomers in Him, and we overcome by the Blood of the Lamb. Signs, wonders, and miracles are sure to come, for we believe in Him who sent us to do all things through His invested power. If it is impossible, it is doable with the Lord working through our faithful hands of creativity. Being humbled, repented, and praying for Thy Kingdom to come on earth, we believe our land will be healed as promised. We look to God, not man, as a lost Nation seeking after His knowledge, wisdom, love, and grace. For the Lord is the Author and the Finisher of our faith, we wait on His glorious reign, having no fear, and putting away all negativity.

We pray for our President, as we are called to do. Heavenly Father, we come before you as your Children humbled through the spirit you gave us. We lift up to you our Nation, and this entire world in which you created as a whole. Have mercy on us; forgive us of all our sins. Let evil not prevail over us, keep your shield of protection around us and guard us with your Angels. Let us have peace and may love always overcome hate. Speak unto the hearts of your people and let us do your will over our own. We pray for our appointed leaders, because we know that you are in control of the elected outcomes. Our President's greater purpose in you Lord Births the need for our prayers this moment. May he be blessed with wisdom, patience, and understanding, in order to meet the requirements of this Nation. Be with him and us all at every moment, and let your will be done in the earth according to your purposeful promise for us all. In Jesus name we pray, Amen.

As the year 3016 comes near, we are responsible for creating the futuristic world next year.

One thousand years is yet one day, and the present year passes away. In a blink time flies by, and memories of yesterday are soon to die. The world as we know it now will be no more, and we will see what heaven has for us in store. With all the brilliance our minds hold, there is something greater happening that no intelligence could ever know. Having imaginations grander than the young, the Lord still keeps secret many things to come. Be full of cheer having a spirit of expectancy, go out into the world and spread the good news with urgency.

Knowing that all of our desires will be given to us for free, we ask and receive all things using our Kingdom key. Remembering that there is nothing impossible, we step up as the Chosen Ones A.K.A. the Unstoppable. As the Saints with all power in our hands, the Kingdom will unfold on earth as we command. Let all of the old things pass away, and the New World to come have its day. He shines before us in all of His glory, the reign of the Son, revealing His story. Being once blind and could not see, the Light of the Lord is ever before me. And though you are deaf refusing to hear, His love is whispering thoughts into your ears.

We cannot make any day or night fall from the sky, nor can we wake ourselves up when we have been called or forced into slumber. We who are in Christ have eternal life and we have in our hands the Kingdom to come, but God is still on the throne and His judgment is upon us. Let us come together from every creed in every nation united as the Church. We are to set the example to the world on what it means to love the Lord and walk as Christ did. Let us not think more highly of ourselves than we ought to, for the greater in us is more when we are weak.

Now we see the bigger picture, it was not about man versus woman, Democrat against Republican, or even blue lives against black lives. It is about good and evil, right or wrong, the wealthy and needy, to help we start loving our enemies and neighbors, and stop being selfish and greedy. We are called as the Chosen Generation, the Saints to judge this world and build it up to edify the Kingdom of God. WAKE UP! Awaken from the slumber of flesh and live in the New Spirit World of Paradise. As Children we are called forth, the seeds of Abraham, the Mighty Nation of God from all nations. Claim the inheritance and take it by force.

I announced that I will run for public office in the near future using social media and grew a following based off of sharing journal posts online. The message has been received well by many and shunned by others. My policies and procedures will be shared for creation purposes, everything of good report, and your heart's desire will be manifested. There will also be a new party created for the people, and by the spirit. It is accepting of all people, and we stand for non-judgment gracious favor, and unification of those who stand for righteousness and doing everything in proper order. Have no worries, this is all in my book that is coming to an airport near you, (Hillary Clinton debate joke).

One of the things on my agenda of change is creating a New Party. If you want to join a New Party made in Heaven, a party that joins all people into the same body, having the same mind when it comes to creating a perfect union, promoting the welfare of those in need with charity, building mansions, solar bubbles, glastic refineries, clean energy plants, a futuristic world of 3,016, using every resource in this world to sustain life in and on every continental crevasse, feeding all people with a system that does not require the use of money, thumbprint scanning, allowing every household an allotment at wealthy status to shop for food, and clothes and life needs, the party will be called the CHURCH!!.

If you have a body you are the Church, we are made up of all people of every creed, denomination, and none, ethnicity, culture, and religion, who are united as One people in the body of Christ. Those in this party have been called to attend the Marriage Party in Heaven and will live forever in the Kingdom of God. The tree of life is offered to us, and we have a job to do as Saints creating the New World, ALL of our dreams and desires will be granted, and we will do all things impossible through Christ. As the Church, we are Overcomers of this world, and we make ourselves at home as if the Kingdom has already come.

Demons and evil speaking oppressors are in our submission, and we call things that are not yet here into existence. In using all-natural resources to the fullest of the created functions, we make gasoline, ropes, clothing, body care products, food, stronger than steel products from hemp for buildings and vehicles, plus many other resources to supply our needs for the Kingdom in every nation. We remove labels from government documents and no longer separate from each other on applications and such by our former hyphens of division. There will be no mention and legal acceptance of the hearing, saying or writing _____-American, and no more white and black and all other colors of separation. Ethnicity is not a factor, because we are all God's children red and yellow included, being precious in His sight. Instead we will only be able to check Americans, or Non-Americans, and eventually we will drop that label and substitute it with the Church and the State. The Church is the body of Christ, and the State is the statue of liberating man in the flesh. One has damnation, and the other salvation. You are free to live out your choice accordingly, but know you are being watched and recorded in the book of life.

In summary, digital technologies will make the political process better if we upgrade our current voting methods to match the advancements we have made over the years. For example, we can use the technology we already have in place to vote online on a secured government voting website. The stench of fear keeps us stagnant, and unable to move forward. We are liberated and free to take control of our political system. Let us keep the Preamble in remembrance. We the People of the United States, in Order to form a more perfect Union, establish Justice, insure domestic Tranquility, provide for the common defense, promote the general Welfare, and secure the Blessings of Liberty to ourselves and our Posterity, do ordain and establish this

Constitution for the United States of America. With that being said, the power is in our hands to make this great Nation what it should be. It is not the digital technologies in control, but the people behind the system. We are not to get weary in our well doing, but be steadfast and unmovable, because the greatness in us is more when we seem to be weakened.

We are embarking on a New Millennium, and the technology we presently have will be far more advanced in the years to come. The future is in our hands, and we will make this world a better place for the generations to come. A thousand years is as yesterday and look at how far we have come in such a short time. Just imagine what it will be like on earth one thousand years from now, if we can see the vision, we can make it a reality. In creating a New System, with a New Party of likeminded individuals from all backgrounds called the Church, we can turn all impossibilities into all things possible. Since we are called to be Saints, and to live and reign with Christ one thousand years, we are responsible for doing the Kingdom work that we are called to do. We have mansions to build, people to care for, and a world ready to be healed. Instead of despising technology, we embrace it as the way of the future. We are one world, one love, and that is all we need to realize to overcome the evil and hate that is soon to be forgotten.

Chapter 6

The Promise of prophecy fulfilled

We have the anthem of our Nation written by Moses, which calls for us to be forever one in the Lord God our Creator. Let us not forget to give our ears in spirit as the Heavens speak, and to let the earth hear the words of His mouth. May His teachings drop as the rain, and speech distill as the dew like gentle rain upon tender grass, and like showers upon the herb. For we proclaim the name of the Lord, ascribing greatness to our God! The Rock, his work is perfect, for all his ways are justice. A God of faithfulness and without iniquity, just and upright is He.

They have dealt corruptly with him; they are no longer his children because they are blemished; they are a crooked and twisted generation. Do you thus repay the LORD, you foolish and senseless people? Is not He your father, who created you, who made you and established you? Remember the days of old; consider the years of many generations; ask your father, and he will show you, your elders, and they will tell you. When the Most High gave to the nations their inheritance, when he divided mankind, he fixed the borders of the peoples according to the number of the sons of God. But the LORD's portion is his people, Jacob his allotted heritage. He found him in a desert land, and in the howling waste of the wilderness; he encircled him, he cared for him,

He kept him as the apple of his eye. Like an eagle that stirs up its nest, that flutters over its young, spreading out its wings, catching them, bearing them on its pinions, the LORD alone guided him, no foreign god was with him. He made him ride on the high places of the land, and he ate the produce of the field, and he suckled him with honey out of the rock, and oil out of the flinty rock. Curds from the herd, and milk from the flock, with fat[3] of lambs, rams of Bashan and goats, with the very finest[4] of the wheat— and you drank foaming wine made from the blood of the grape. But Jesurun grew fat, and kicked; you grew fat, stout, and sleek; then he forsook

God who made him and scoffed at the Rock of his salvation. They stirred him to jealousy with strange gods; with abominations they provoked him to anger. They sacrificed to demons that were no gods, to gods they had never known, to new gods that had come recently, whom your fathers had never dreaded. You were unmindful of the Rock that bore[5] you, and you forgot the God who gave you birth. The LORD saw it and spurned them, because of the provocation of his sons and his daughters. And he said, I will hide my face from them; I will see what their end will be, for they are a perverse generation, children in whom is no faithfulness. They have made me jealous with what is no god; they have provoked me to anger with their idols. So, I will make them jealous with those who are no people; I will provoke them to anger with a foolish nation. For [f]a fire is kindled by my anger, and it burns to the depths of Sheol, devours the earth and its increase and sets on fire the foundations of the mountains. And I will heap disasters upon them; I will spend my arrows on them; they shall be wasted with hunger and devoured by plague and poisonous pestilence; I will send the teeth of beasts against them, with the venom of things that crawl in the dust. Outdoors the sword shall bereave, and indoors terror, for young man and woman alike, the nursing child with the man of gray hairs. I would have said, "I will cut them to pieces; I will wipe them from human memory," had I not feared provocation by the enemy, lest their adversaries should misunderstand, lest they should say, "Our hand is triumphant, it was not the LORD who did all this." For they are a nation void of counsel, and there is [o]no understanding in them. If they were wise, they would understand this;

they would discern their latter end! How could one have chased a thousand, and two have put ten thousand to flight, unless their Rock [s]had sold them, and the LORD had given them up? For their rock is not as our Rock; our enemies are by themselves.

For their vine comes from the vine of Sodom and from the fields of Gomorrah; their grapes are grapes of poison; their clusters are bitter; their wine is the poison of serpents and the cruel venom of asps. Is not this laid up in store with me, sealed up in my treasuries? Vengeance is mine, and recompense, for the time when their foot shall slip; for the day of their calamity is at hand, and their doom comes swiftly.' For the LORD will vindicate his people and have compassion on his servants, when he sees that their power is gone and there is none remaining, bond or free. Then he will say, Where are their gods, the rock in which they took refuge, who ate the fat of their sacrifices and drank the wine of their drink offering? Let them rise up and help you; let them be your protection! See now that I, even I, am he, and there is no god beside me; I kill, and I make alive; I wound, and I heal;

and there is none that can deliver out of my hand.

For I lift up my hand to heaven and swear, As I live forever, if I sharpen my flashing sword and my hand takes hold on judgment, I will take vengeance on my adversaries and will repay those who hate me. I will make my arrows drunk with blood, and my sword shall devour flesh— with the blood of the slain and the captives, from the long-haired heads of the enemy.' "Rejoice with him, O heavens;[2] bow down to him, all gods, for he avenges the blood of his children-and takes vengeance on his adversaries. He repays those who hate him and cleanses his people's land."

Moses recited these words as a song to the people, and they heard him. When he finished speaking to all of Israel he said to them, " Take to heart all of the words by which I am warning you of today, that you may command them to your children, that they may be careful to do all the words of this law. For it is no empty word for you, but your very life, and by this word you shall live long in the land that you are going over the Jordan to possess.

We as African Americans share the history of captivity in America for four hundred years the same as the Israelites from Egypt. And, as an honor to that heritage I share the words to the Black National Anthem, may these words unite us as a people of who love without condition.

Lift ev'ry voice and sing

Also known as: The Black National Anthem

Lift ev'ry voice and sing,

Till earth and heaven ring.

Ring with the harmonies of Liberty;

Let our rejoicing rise,

High as the list'ning skies,

Let it resound loud as the rolling sea.

Sing a song full of the faith that the dark past has

taught us,

Sing a song full of the hope that the present has

brought us;

Facing the rising sun of our new day begun,

Let us march on till victory is won.

Stony the road we trod,

Bitter the chast'ning rod,

Felt in the days when hope unborn had died;

Yet with a steady beat,

Have not our weary feet,

Come to the place for which our fathers sighed?

We have come over a way that with tears has been

watered,

We have come, treading our path through the blood

of the slaughtered,

Out from the gloomy past,

Till now we stand at last

Where the white gleam of our bright star is cast.

God of our weary years,

God of our silent tears,

Thou who has brought us thus far on the way;

Thou who has by Thy might,

Led us into the light,

Keep us forever in the path, we pray.

Lest our feet stray from the places, our God, where

we met Thee,

Lest our hearts, drunk with the wine of the world, we

forget Thee,

Shadowed beneath thy hand,

May we forever stand,

True to our God,

True to our native land.

It is now and not tomorrow, for only
today is promised. Whether we are ready or
not it is coming, so we push through it like

contractions. We see the land before us swelling and producing and have already witnessed the fatness thereof. Let us come into the full knowledge of the truth, allowing the wisdom of what was once so empower us and take fruit. When we look back at the life of Moses and see that before he closed his eyes taking his last breath, He saw the Paradise awaiting. Still it has always been there, and it has never left. Let us see it too. Though our eyes are blinded to the beauty ever before us it does not mean it exists not, but only that we have been distracted. But now, we focus our eyes on the prize in front of us, and we do not lose hope.

There is no weariness as we continue to endure through the home stretch, and at the finish we all win. Having our eyes open in the spirit seeing the glory of God in the sky's horizon, we look up with anticipation at the Kingdom's coming. As the atmosphere changes and the presence of the Lord is upon us, we see the Heaven's open as a baby crowning during delivery. The excitement and joy that comes with the receiving of this gift makes for all the pain and suffering felt previously to shift. Now we hold this great responsibility in our hands, and we must follow all the steps as planned.

As Moses stood looking out of the window before his death, he saw the promise land out before him, taking his last breath he walked in. Moses lead the Israelites out of captivity where they were slaves for four hundred years, and for forty years they wandered in the wilderness never seeing the land of milk and honey as their children did. The same rings true for Martin Luther King Jr., who lead a people of all races into a peaceful movement of union for freedom. As King looked out on the mountaintop, he too saw the promise land, and his words spoke of the truth that it is here for us to walk in. Coming together as friends in love despite our differences opens the atmosphere for blessings.

Chapter 7

Recognizing the true enemy

Do not question if the road is straight and narrow, because it is. Those who are full of deceit and fraud, are sons of the devil, an enemy of Righteousness. They do not stop being crooked and deny the straight ways of the Lord. In all of our ways we must acknowledge Christ, and He will make our paths straight. We do not turn to the left or the right but do turn away from evil. In this administration we hear many say the Left did this, or the Right said that, but if we keep our eyes on Jesus in all of our ways we will not be distracted. Let the voice cry out in the wilderness and proclaim, "MAKE READY

THE WAY OF THE LORD, MAKE HIS PATHS STRAIGHT!" As our feet make straight paths, lame limbs will pop back into joint, and be healed.

Let us not think more highly of ourselves than we should, claiming to be a genius or the smartest is not walking in humility. We are called to live modest and humble lives, and to exalt others over ourselves. Proverbs 3:7 tells us not to be wise in our own eyes, but to fear the Lord and turn away from evil.

The Lord says that He arouses Righteousness, and He smooths out the way. Isaiah 45:13 goes on to say the Holy City will be built, and the exiles set free without any payment or reward. We concentrate too much on the how and who of things getting paid, when the Word says no payment is required. The birds in the air do not exchange money, and neither shall we. God expects us to care for each other, especially the least. As He cares for the birds, don't you think that His people are more precious than them?

Haven't you heard that to whom much is given much is required, and that the wealth of the wicked is held up for the righteous? Jesus is the same today as He was then, and as He said before He will say it again. When approached, the story went, "Good teacher," he asked, "what must I do to inherit eternal life?" [18]"Why do you call me good?" Jesus answered. "No one is good- except God alone. [19]You know the commandments: 'You shall not murder, you shall not commit adultery, you shall not steal, you shall not give false testimony, you shall not defraud, honor your father and mother.'" [20]"Teacher," he declared, "all these I have kept since I was a boy." [21]Jesus looked at him and loved him. "One thing you lack," he said. "Go, sell everything you have and give to the poor, and you will have treasure in heaven. Then come, follow me." [22]At this the man's face fell. He went away sad, because he had great wealth. [23]Jesus looked around and said to his disciples, "How hard it is for the rich to enter the kingdom of God!" [24]The disciples were amazed at his words. But Jesus said again, "Children, how hard it is to enter the kingdom of God! [25]It is easier for a camel to go through the eye of a needle than for someone who is rich to enter the kingdom of God."

Our President is elected into office by the hand of God, not for Trump's purpose but for the will of the Lord. Entering into Heaven is hard for the rich, because the treasures gained in the world are difficult to part with. But we must detach ourselves from this world and all things in it.

As a fool gives full vent to his spirit, wisdom knows to be quiet is better. Everyone who hears the words of God and obeys wisely builds his house on the rock. The rock is where we build the church, and the gates of hell will not prevail against us. The Lord is our rock, our fortress and our deliverer. We take refuge under His shield sounding the horn of salvation, calling on the name of the Lord with a triumphant shout of praise, we are saved from our enemies. Embracing wise instruction, we stand in awe of the all-knowing God trembling in fear. The wisdom we receive from above is pure, peaceful, gentle, open to reason, full of mercy and good fruits, impartial and sincere. We are to be found blameless and innocent as children of God without blemish in the midst of a crooked and twisted generation, and we shine our lights among them as directed. The Lord gives wisdom generously to all who ask without reproach, let us lack for nothing. We have been told what the Lord hates, and know what an abomination to Him is: haughty eyes, a lying tongue, and hands that shed innocent blood, a heart that devises wicked plans, feet that make haste to run to evil, a false witness who breathes out lies, and one who sows discord among brothers. Having haughty eyes being arrogant, vain, with a superior attitude, is as pride coming before the fall of man. For these things we ask for forgiveness and repent, let us not think more highly of ourselves than we ought to think. Being made humble is a process of change that comes with surrendering. We are to do nothing out of selfish ambition or vain conceit, but in humility consider others better than us. Not looking out for our own interest, but we look out for the interest of the least around us. We should not say that we are the best of anything when God has created us to be better together. We are called to live in harmony with one another, to associate with the lowest, and to never be wise in our own sight. We know that, "No one can serve two masters, for either he will hate the one and love the other, or he will be devoted to the one and despise the other. We cannot serve God and money. Therefore, we must look carefully at how we walk, not as unwise but as wise, making the best use of the time, because the days are evil. Therefore, do not be foolish, but understand what the will of the Lord is.

President Donald trump campaign slogan said that a lion does not lose sleep over the opinion of his sheep, MAKE AMERICA GREAT AGAIN! And, the red and blue image of the lion jumping over the republican and democrat symbols, the 2016 message mirrors my views in 2008. However, it contradicts the word of God, because as Christ Jesus is the Lamb of God and the Lion of Judah, and He loses sleep over His Sheep. Matter of fact, He leaves the 99 for the One Lost Sheep, and rejoices after it is found.

Do not be deceived but stay sober and watch out! Our adversary the devil prowls around like a roaring lion seeking to devour people. The Lion of Judah comforts our weeping, and Overcomes so He can open the Book, and its seven seals. There is only one Lion, and it is the Lord. And, at the Sound of the seventh Angel loud voices shout out, "THE KINGDOM OF THE WORLD HAS BECOME THE KINGDOM OF OUR LORD AND OF HIS CHRIST; AND HE WILL REIGN FOREVER AND EVER."

I shared the journal below in 2008, it is from my retired book, The Sun's Love Clothes My Soul.

Is our Nation united or divided?

by

Godstar

May 2, 2008 at 2:35 PM

Is our Nation united or divided?

Liberal v. Conservative: Why is this Nation so

divided between these two groups?

A DIVIDED NATION WILL FALL!!

Maybe a lion should come and eat the

donkey and scare the elephant into a heart-

attack!! Then the new lion mascot for the

United Country would take over the world

and rule as the Kingdom of Heaven!!

The Republican Party was born in the early 1850's by anti-slavery activists and individuals who believed that government should grant western lands to settlers free of charge. In 1856, the Republicans became a national party when John C. Fremont was nominated for President under the slogan: "Free soil, free labor, free speech, free men, Fremont." Even though they were considered a "third party" because the Democrats and Whigs represented the two-party system at the time, Fremont received 33% of the vote. Four years later, Abraham Lincoln became the first Republican to win the White House.

Ever wondered what the story was

behind these two famous party animals? The now-famous Democratic donkey was first associated with Democrat Andrew Jackson's 1828 presidential campaign. His opponents called him a jackass (a donkey), and Jackson decided to use the image of the strong-willed animal on his campaign posters. Later, cartoonist Thomas Nast used the Democratic donkey in newspaper cartoons and made the symbol famous.

Nast invented another famous symbol—the Republican elephant. In a cartoon that appeared in Harper's Weekly in 1874, Nast drew a donkey clothed in lion's skin, scaring away all the animals at the zoo. One of those animals, the elephant, was labeled "The

Republican Vote." That's all it took for the elephant to become associated with the Republican Party.

Democrats today say the donkey is smart and brave, while Republicans say the elephant is strong and dignified.

I say the lion is the BEST!!

President Trumps acceptance speech after being elected mirrored many of my beliefs that I shared in my books and online over the last ten years. I'll take it as confirmation instead of offense. As far as I know, those who wrote for this

Administration had good intentions, so my feelings are not hard. So, let it be so, and we will come from all places with ideas for the new world of the future. Let our dreams be heard, and the desires made so into reality through our hand's creation. We will come together as one people and establish a government of right-standing benefitting all people equally.   As we work hard with every able body we will build and supply our needs sufficiently and abundantly. Allowing the flow of trillions from the new economic policies we will build and make things in order to uplift the Kingdom of Heaven on earth. As we do these things to benefit the poor, widows, and orphans more so than the wealthy and already established we find favor in the eyes of God. The quality of life should not only improve for all Americans, but for every being in the world. For, to whom much is given, much is required. Our blessings are due to fall on all, the just and the unjust. And, the inheritance of Abraham is overdue to the generations of the fallen. The building of roads, highways, bridges, tunnels, airports, and railways are waiting the applicants of excess, and Space Force needs my Solar Bubble to Hubble through the Galactic Superhighways of Space. No unemployment sounds like a winner to me, as it does to you too. Rescuing the children from failing schools by running away (allowing the parents to pick another school), creates a problem down the line in economic development. The neighborhoods in failing school districts suffer from poverty and they will continue to decline without direct intervention. A love a child village program would be of better value and bring more jobs to low-income areas. Send a lifeboat after everyone scatters with lifejackets on, lets transform the worst neighborhoods to safe resorts of escape. It is wonderful to have a platform as a messenger of God, and to be able to speak what's in my heart in my free country. As you promised, the repeal of Lyndon Johnson's amendment that threatened religious institutions with a loss of their tax-exempt status if we openly advocated our political views and protecting free speech for all people is welcomed. As we believe in ourselves and know that ALL things are possible to those who believe, we will accomplish the great things God has established for us.

Dreams are the windows for our souls to peer through, be prepared to open the glass and let the wind move you as envisioned. Together we will bring forth the Kingdom of Heaven on Earth. The victory belongs to Jesus, for all people, the time has come.

President Trump also said that we must break free from the petty politics of the past, and God says that the Chains are broken, and the past is thrown into the sea of forgetfulness through repentance. As the nation of believers, dreamers and go-getters, we will not be stopped by the cynical, censorships, or even the critics. More than believing in America, we believe in God and knowing that the people were ready for change by electing a woman, we accept that the story was written before the vote. We do not rely on people, but on the spirit that leads us unto place of promise. We shall rise as the Light begins and show our brightness to the entire world. Declaring the truth, we shout out with a voice of triumph proclaiming that Christ lives in us. With the greatness in us we overcome this whole earth in judgment and stand strong in the condemnation of our opponent. Do not shout that you are with her, him, or recite that I'm with you, but let us all say with pride that we are with God. May all our voices be heard, and all our dreams come true as promised by the Only One who can accomplish greatness and heal our whole world. In weakness we receive the strength of God, being humble brings the blessings, our safety umbrellas as His protection, and greater is He that is in us all. The blessings of Abraham befall on us, and the peace of Christ rest our minds in stillness.

The end brings forth drawn curtains as the song plays haunting melodies of repetitive blows of reckoning. We look on with heavy hearts and mourn the lost hope of love in a dark world of gloom. Let there not be trouble or rumors of treacherous murmurings. Our worries will not be counted among the shameful as signs of weakness, for we know not the meaning of true faith without instruction. Conquering all by the hand, instead of building up the spirit of man through creation, we turnaround. Having all things impossible available to us by the drive to work out our visions through divine inspiration. Knowing that true understanding of the law works with the ability to bring order and justice to all people equally.

The balancing of checks surplus through increased branches of sharing; resulting in overstocks of flowing blessings exchanged through fair markets. The wealth of the wicked is handed over to the poor, and the riches are bestowed upon the whole earth.

Do not be dismayed and realize that the greater in us is more than enough to conquer the matters of this world, for Christ has overcame it and gave us His spirit to do the same.

Having repented and humbled ourselves as a child in submission, we give up our ways for the way of Righteousness.

Knowing our tongues are wicked vessels of flesh in the matter of facts, we seal up our lips with slow speech and girdled tongues. Careful not to esteem ourselves more highly than we ought to, but making ourselves low as Christ did for us, becoming servants of the Most High God. Giving glory to His name, we fall to our knees and cry out ABBA,

ABBA come near us!! For we need you to heal our land, and bring us back to right standing, oh God.

Forgive us of all the things we did knowingly and unknowingly to offend you and keep us from sinning against you. Surrendering all we have at your feet, fill us up with your presence and take us up to Heaven. Fall down on us as the earth crumples with laboring pains of new birth and bring us together as one land of people in who we were all created in.

There is no division only communion in love made perfect, and through this death of one many are saved into new life. Having been resurrected with the dead in Christ we stand as the Chosen People of redeemed promises and claim our inheritance boldly. This land is ours, and wherever our feet touch we bless it bountifully with fruition. The harvest is nigh for the time has come, let's eat and be merry. The Kingdom of Heaven is in our Hands!

The song plays as the President and First lady dance and sing along to Frank Sinatra's, "My Way."

The lyrics as follows...

MY WAY

Frank Sinatra

And now the end is near

So I face the final curtain

My friend, I'll say it clear

I'll state my case of which I'm certain

I've lived a life that's full

I've traveled each and every highway

And more, much more than this

I did it my way

Regrets, I've had a few

But then again, too few to mention

I did what I had to do

And saw it through without exception

I planned each charted course

Each careful step along the byway

Oh, and more, much more than this

I did it my way

Yes, there were times, I'm sure you knew

When I bit off more than I could chew

But through it all when there was doubt

I ate it up and spit it out

I faced it all and I stood tall

And did it my way

        I've loved, I've laughed and cried

        I've had my fails, my share of losing

        And now as tears subside

        I find it all so amusing

        To think I did all that

        And may I say, not in a shy way

        Oh, no, no not me

        I did it my way

        For what is a man, what has he got

        If not himself, then he has not

        To say the things he truly feels

        And not the words he would reveal

        The record shows I took the blows

        And did it my way

Let us not provoke the Lord of our generation by going astray in our hearts, may His ways be known to us. Not our will, but His will be done. We are not foolish, so we understand the will of the Lord. He leads the humble in the ways of Righteousness, and He teaches us His way. We humble ourselves under the mighty hand of God, and we will be exalted in time. We have no fears or cares, because every anxiety is cast on Him. Our lives are free from the love of money, and we live contently knowing that we are not forsaken. By the narrow gate we enter! The wide gate that leads to the easy way out opens to destruction, and most end up there. But, the hard way of life that few make it out of is narrow yet rewarding. Our ways are not the ways of the Lord, because His thoughts surpass the capacity of our mind. His plans are known to us, our welfare is thought of and he keeps us from evil while giving us a hopeful future. Jesus Christ is the way, the truth, and the life. No one makes it into Heaven except through Christ, and it is easier for a camel to get through an eye of a needle than it is for a rich man to make it in. Be careful who you follow, because they might not be willing to let go of everything they own to go to paradise. What is required of us is to be just, to love and show kindness, and walk with God humbly. Every prideful possession, lust of the flesh, longing of the eyes is worldly, and not from God. We who will live forever abiding in Him do only His will, never having our way as a sacrifice. We patiently tend to the needs of others with care, holding no jealousy and without bragging have no arrogance in the acts of our love. If there be any boasting it will gladly be of our weaknesses, so that we may be filled with the power of Christ. His grace is more than enough for us, and His power is made perfect in weakness. If we are doing God's will it will be known that the teaching is from God and not by our own authority. The time is here when people will not listen to sound teaching, because they want to pursue their own personal passions outside of God. We will not be held captive by philosophy or empty deceit being bonded to tradition, and nothing within this world will keep us from the truth of Christ. We are not too proud to ask for forgiveness, or to say that we are sorry. If we say that we have not sinned then we are calling God a liar, and His word is not in our hearts. For all of us have sinned and we fall short of the glory, but by grace we are pardoned. The wicked must change his ways and his thoughts unto righteousness, return to the Lord and He will forgive with abundant compassion. If we confess our sins, He is faithful and just to forgive us and cleanse us from all unrighteousness. Those of us who are broken and crushed in spirit are close to the Lord. We pray for peace, and His security and love for us all. For the sake of the Kingdom we will not keep quiet, the silence of past years muffled as church hymns behind the walls come out as a shout in the streets. Righteousness dawns brightly, and salvation holds up the flaming torch. We are pilgrims in the land of Zion dwelling with the Lord in our midst, and in the faithful city of Jerusalem, the holy mountain the Lord host. Proclaiming repentance of sins, bestowing forgiveness in the name of Jesus to all Nations from Jerusalem out. As a people who lives seem not to matter, we are not orphaned, and our Father restores our health as He heals our wounds. Our salvation has come, the reward has presented us with the honor of being called The Holy People,   The Redeemed of the Lord, we are Sought Out, and A City Not Forsaken. We the people of God are surrounded by Him always and forever as the mountains surround Jerusalem. We do not love money and pull out the root that chokes charity. All nations shall come together at the throne of the Lord, and no one will be stubborn and follow the evil of their hearts.

Balancing the budget of this world, managing the ins and outs of production we are held accountable with tax. Mindfully connecting with like minds, we counter hate with love and resistance. Being careful not to rough up feathers we peacefully express ourselves with living words of power, and this smooths out the spread of colors showing love.

There has never been a president like Donald Trump, he says it like it is. Repent!

Let us consider our words and let them be used to edify and uplift people. Be careful not to speak curses, because the judgment comes back to come true for the accuser. There is corruption, and this country needs godly leadership. The house is divided, it will not stand, and the falling is happening before our very own eyes. The investigations have been no stop, and all things done in secret will come out. The Light shines in the darkness and expels the evil in truth. Obstructing justice in collusion as the love of money shows its side, may the proceedings be favorable in reversing the flow of current exchange from the wicked to the righteous. Having respect for each other while being respectful, let every country come together as one world. Putting aside our egos we show concern for our fellow man, and we create joyous occasions so that laughter increases our lifespans. We share the knowledge of truth and the wisdom of God, so that no one lacks the good news. Knowing that our words are life or death, we speak only things of a good report that bring eternal life. As we guard our tongues, we always girdle our mouths with the truth. Our refuge is in the Lord, and we do not trust in man. Blowing on the horn of our salvation, shielded **in the fortress of God, standing on the rock of deliverance, we are held in the strength of His refuge.**

We are confident in the Lord and will not be taken by the stumbling of foot. Even in the middle of troubling times, we walk with preserved lives, the Lord hand is stretched out against the plots of the enemy, and His right hand delivers us. God opposes the proud, and He gives even more grace to the humble. Blessings come to the one that stays steady when tried, after withstanding the test the crown of life is received, this is promised to everyone who loves the Lord. We have no fears, because God is with us to deliver us from every trap.   All of us born of God overcomes this world, and the victory in Christ is our faith. By faith we heal the sick and release the shut-in. Those afflicted, torn, and oppressed are welcomed, and there will be no lack. We are called to take care of the Lord's people as well as our enemies, the wealth of the wicked will pour out to the less fortunate. The orphaned, widowed, and the sick are our main priorities, we are the Advocates of Christ. We are the guardians of the earth and promise to keep the environment in spiritual atmospheric settings.

 As the word reads and lives, let it abide in us so that on judgment day we are called worthy to be His Sheep.

15 When they had finished eating, Jesus said to Simon Peter, "Simon son of John, do you love me more than these?"

"Yes, Lord," he said, "you know that I love you."

Jesus said, "Feed my lambs."

16 Again Jesus said, "Simon son of John, do

you love me?"

He answered, "Yes, Lord, you know that I love you."

Jesus said, "Take care of my sheep."

17 The third time he said to him, "Simon son of John, do you love me?"

Peter was hurt because Jesus asked him the third time, "Do you love me?" He said, "Lord, you know all things; you know that I love you."

Jesus said, "Feed my sheep. 18 Very truly I tell you, when you were younger you dressed yourself and went where you wanted; but when you are old you will stretch out your hands, and someone else will dress you and lead you where you do not want to go." 19

Jesus said this to indicate the kind of death

by which Peter would glorify God. Then he

said to him, "Follow me!"

Chapter 8

Contradictions to the teachings

A journal entry post of mine from November 2016.

The Anti-Christ is spiritual wickedness in High Places, one who speaks contradictions to the teachings of Christ, and brings with Him followers who portray themselves as sheep, but underneath are wolves in fake clothes. Jesus said to us come all who are weary and rest, the opposer says go away all who are in need.

The Lord says give, the enemy says take. Jesus says provide food, water, shelter, clothes, heal the sick, and go to the prisoners, the adversary despises charity

and wants to lock up everyone who offends him. Christ our Lord says love your neighbors as yourself, and He explained who our neighbor is- (the next country), the suppressor says, "Build a wall to keep the neighbors out!" God says love your enemies, and pray for those who persecute you, the devil says destroy them and their children.

You who are called to be one of the Saints, decide for yourself if it be the will of God or the will of man this election....

If any of you has a grievance against another, how dare he go to law before the unrighteous instead of before the saints! **2<u>Do you not</u> <u>know</u> <u>that</u> <u>the</u> <u>saints</u> <u>will</u> <u>judge</u> <u>the</u> <u>world?</u> <u>And</u> <u>if</u> <u>you</u> <u>are to</u> <u>judge</u> <u>the</u> <u>world,</u> <u>are you not competent</u> <u>to</u> <u>judge trivial</u> <u>cases?</u> 3Do you not know that we will judge angels? How much more the things of this life! 1 Corinthians 6:1-3**

Therefore, if thine enemy hunger, feed him; if he thirst, give him drink: for in so doing thou shalt heap coals of fire on his head. Romans 12:20

35 For I was a hungered, and ye gave me meat: I was thirsty, and ye gave me drink: I was a stranger, and ye took me in:

36 Naked, and ye clothed me: I was sick, and ye visited me: I was in prison, and ye came unto me.

37 Then shall the righteous answer him, saying, Lord, when saw we thee a hungered, and fed thee? or thirsty, and gave thee drink?

38 When saw we thee a stranger, and took thee in? or naked, and clothed thee?

39 Or when saw we thee sick, or in prison, and came unto thee?

40 And the King shall answer and say unto them, Verily I say unto you, inasmuch as ye have done it unto one of the least of these my brethren, ye have done it unto me. Matthew 25:35-40 KJV

Many watched as President Trump proposed a budget cutting the meals on wheels program. Knowing that the service fed the elderly many of who are widowed, it was a slap to the face of Jesus. As the Lord forgives, His cheek is turned but we pray that no more licks be laid. Our Savior has endured enough pain, and His ways are set before us as a tablet. The Light to the Lamp of His Feet guides us through the steps to follow into His Gates. Blocking housing for those who Christ promised a place of dwelling is self-serving and not doing a good service. As the Lord shelters us let us shelter the homeless, leaving no one alone or hungry.

Surely the Lord wants us to feed His people, take care of the widows, sick, and shut-in, only the devil himself would try to stop that.

We are called to serve one another as Christ served us. He gave up His body for the Church, so we must sacrifice our flesh to live in the spirit. If we served ourselves and did only our will, we would be selfish, God's will is for us to be selfless. In Christ, we all work together as One family in His body using our talents and gifts for building up the Kingdom. The Church is His body, and we are to obey the head to operate in the will of the Lord.

Trump has been put into power as our leader, and Obama was not the Anti-Christ by far. God said that He establishes all authorities, and all that exist have been put in place by Him. I did not make that up, it is the word of God. Obama has tried to provide health care to all people and that is in the will of God, Trump wants to take that away, because he is working against the will of God. I know that Obama has made some mistakes, that happens when you try to please the world and God at the same time. It makes you lukewarm, and that is a problem. Trump is not in the middle, he is not hot in knowing the word, but cold in the things of God. The scripture is clear when it says that God puts the authority figures in place, Satan has no authority over God, and he cannot do anything unless God allows it. The whole world does not wonder at President Obama, but the world is dumbfounded by Trump rising up to this level of power as the scripture illustrates. It is clearly a revelation of Trump in every sentence, and not Obama. You cannot show me a scripture in the bible that proves that God is not involved, for the Lord is the Ruler over all things good and bad.

 I form the light, and create darkness: I make peace, and create evil: I the LORD do all these *things*.

Isaiah 45:7

Let everyone be subject to the governing authorities, for there is no authority except that which God has established. The authorities that exist have been established by God. Romans 13:1

Jesus says that we are to love our enemies, do good to those who hate us, and bless those who curse us. The Lord says do not take revenge but leave room for God's wrath, for it is written: "Vengeance belongs to me; I will repay, says the Lord." Donald Trump says, "when people wrong you go after them, because it is a good feeling and because other people will see you doing it. I always get even." Jesus tells us to love your neighbor as yourself. Trump plans on building a wall on our southern border, and he wants to make Mexico pay for it. Jesus will say to those on His right, "Come you , you who are blessed by my Father; take your inheritance, the kingdom prepared for you since the creation of the world. For I was hungry and you gave me something to eat, I was thirsty and you gave me something to drink, I was a stranger and you invited me in, I needed clothes and you clothed me, I was sick and you looked after me, I was in prison and you came to visit me.' Then the righteous will answer him, 'Lord, when did we see you hungry and feed you, or thirsty and give you something to drink? When did we see you a stranger and invite you in, or needing clothes and clothe you? When did we see you sick or in prison and go to visit you?' The King will reply, 'Truly I tell you, whatever you did for one of the least of these brothers and sisters of mine, you did for me.''

Donald Trump put people on notice that were arriving as refugees that if he wins, they would be going back. Jesus said that those who exalt themselves will be humbled, and those who humble themselves will be exalted. Donald Trump said, "Sorry losers and haters, but my I.Q. is one of the highest- and you all know it! Please do not feel so stupid or insecure, it's not your fault. Jesus told us that He did not come to call the righteous, but sinners to repentance. And, it is written that no one is righteous, not even one. We have all sinned and fallen short of the glory of God, and we are all justified freely by His grace through the redemption from Christ Jesus. Trump asked why does he have to repent and ask for forgiveness if he is not making mistakes? Jesus says blessed are the merciful, for they will be shown mercy. Trump supported water boarding totally, even suggesting expanding the law to contain it. Jesus blessed the meek and said that they will inherit the earth. Donald Trump thinks apologizing is a great thing, but you have to be wrong. He said that he would apologize in the distant future if he is ever wrong. Jesus blessed the peacemakers and said that they will be called the children of God. Trump told us that he could stand in the middle of Fifth Avenue and shoot somebody and still wouldn't lose voters. Jesus told us not to store up treasures for ourselves on earth, where moths and vermin destroy, and where thieves break in and steal. But we are to store up our treasure in Heaven where they cannot be destroyed or stolen. Where our treasure is, so will our heart be there also. According to Trump, part of the beauty of him is that he is very rich. Trump says that when he goes to church and drinks his little wine and eats his little cracker, he guesses that is a form of forgiveness. And, he does this often as possible because he feels cleansed. Jesus said, "this is my body which is given for you; do this in remembrance of Him. This cup is the new covenant in His blood which is poured out for us. Jesus is the savior of our world, and the only one can rely on to make our world good. Trump said that Jesus is somebody that he can think about for security and confidence, so in relying on Christ we can overcome this world. We are instructed to be quick to listen, slow to speak, and slow to become angry, because being angry does not produce the righteousness God desires for us. We know to use words with restraint, and those of us who are even-tempered understand. It is said in the word that, even fools are thought to be wise if they keep silent, but they must hold their tongues. The Lord shows us when we are wrong, in the stillness of quiet He teaches us. And, who the Lord loves He corrects.

As a leader we are required to not act out of selfishness or empty conceit, but in humility consider others as more important than ourselves. We the people rejoice when the righteous increase, and when a wicked man rules we groan. Let us not think more highly of ourselves than we ought to think, judging soundly we will be dealt with by the measure of our faith. We should do our best in presenting ourselves to God for approval, having no shame, we speak the word of truth in love always. In order to be great, we must be willing to serve, those who say they are the greatest must be willing to be the least. As Jesus Christ came not to be served but to serve, and He gave His life as a ransom for us all. So, whatever we wish for others to do for us, we must be willing to do the same for them. Those who cause division and offend have been marked, and we are to avoid such men. There is no need to impress people, and we are not supposed to be selfish but humble. Our leaders should be people capable of trust, who fear God and hate dishonest gain. Our interest are of no importance unless it meets the needs of others. In order for us to live peaceful and quiet lives being holy and godly, we must pray and give thanks for all people especially those in authority. As it pleases God, we lift up President Trump and pray that he aligns his will with the will of God.

As the Vice President Mike Pence shared the story of his personal relationship with Jesus Christ, we wait on the righteous to take a stand. He has studied the red words of Christ and is aware of the falling away from the direction of God. The voices of the

Righteous need to speak out, do not be silent as the world pushes away our prayers. Our loyalty is to God before man, and the stableness of His steady Hands grips us tight unlike the shakiness of being dropped by man.

Yielded powerless in the act of serving others in love, as it was given to us in the act of sacrifice, we serve.

Submitting ourselves as an offering of adoration for the undeserving completion of rectification through redemption by way of His Blood.

As we are a people who love without condition, having the same spirit in us that was in Christ, let it be shown through His love for us as a penance of self-sacrifice.

As He loved us, and gave His life for us, let us love each other

and give up our ways for a better way of

living.

The needs of our brothers and sisters over our own wants

and desires are lifted up, as the will of the

Father was done in Christ obedience.

As death was only the entryway for the Spirit's Comforter to

come, as opened hearts of welcoming He rest

inside of not all yet but some.

Have no frets and worry not, because He comes quickly and

swift to those who forgot.

But, to those who remember and keep the truth bond, hold

on to the Comforter in us His love

abundantly found.

It is an entity not just a man, Satan and all of

his angels...The administration, parties,

and all that backs him along with foreign bodies uniting. The Anti-Christ is spiritual wickedness in High Places that comes speaking contrary to the words of Christ, it is not flesh.

We cannot make any day or night fall from the sky, nor can we wake ourselves up when we have been called or forced into slumber. We who are in Christ have eternal life and we have in our hands the Kingdom to come, but God is still on the throne and His judgment is upon us. Let us come together from every creed in every nation united as the Church.

We are to set the example to the world on what it means to love the Lord and walk as Christ. Let us not think more highly of ourselves than we ought to, for the greater in us is more when we are weak. Now we see the bigger picture, it was not about man versus woman, Democrat against Republican, or even blue lives against black lives. It is about good and evil, right or wrong, the wealthy and needy, to help we start loving our enemies and neighbors, and stop being selfish and greedy.

We are called as the Chosen Generation the Saints to judge this world and build it up to edify the Kingdom of God. WAKE UP!!!! Awaken from the slumber of flesh and live in the New Spirit World of Paradise.

Children I calleth thee forth, the seeds of Abraham, the Mighty Nation of God from

all nations COME FORTH!!! Claim the inheritance and take it by force.

ONE PEOPLE, ONE WORLD, CHRIST REIGN.

Donald Trump's words contradicted the actions of love, which means to give. GIVE, GIVE, GIVE!!! If not, charity we have nothing, love brings unity. Give and it shall be given back, pressed down without measure. History showed us the barbaric methods of taking, the Indians, Africans, Jewish, Hispanic, and any other people there be endured at the hands of greed. We know the voice of righteousness and the strangers voice we will not follow. A rich man can enter the Kingdom, but it is hard for him to give up ALL he has for the poor. For it is true, the love of money is the root to all evil. It shall be plucked and cast into the flames of redemption.

The truth cannot be refuted; accept it for wisdom greater than the simple words of vulgarity which have no substance.

For the love of money is the root of all evil: which while some coveted after, they have erred from the faith, and pierced themselves through with many sorrows. 1Timothy 6:10 KJV

It is better to stay of sober mind and pray for guidance, so the Lord will lead us back to His flock of righteousness. Trump said he loved the uneducated just as the master forbids the slave knowledge, but God wants you to seek wisdom comprehending the knowledge shared. Your mind tells you one thing, but your heart knows the truth. We must overcome the mind with the washing of the word.

The more you give, the more comes back to you, because God is the greatest giver in the universe, and He won't let you out give Him. Go ahead and try. See what happens." Randy Alcorn

"A lack of generosity refuses to acknowledge that your assets are not really yours, but God's." Tim Keller

Seeking permanent tax cuts to benefit mostly the wealthy is not a righteous act, but charity is what we are called to do in love. Were any favors done that were not profitable to this administration in the long run? At tax time we will see if it balances out or not, speaking of taxes will President Trump show his or not? Inventing fake quotes and tweeting when we should all be sleeping, not to mention boasting and lying is the opposite of being Godly. Shouting out fake news media propaganda is only a ploy to deflect the obvious. Rushing to release federal lands for businesses, but still many homeless veterans remain in America, needs reformation. What happened to the promise made at 100 days? There is plenty land here to make sure everyone, especially those that fought for our freedoms have a bed. It is strangely coincidental that the professor who promised campaign dirt on Hillary Clinton might be dead, as it feels like the country is under a mafia style control. Calling for the DOJ to investigate the author of the Times op-ed is a direct violation of our constitutional rights, if the article was not true then Trump should not care.

Having a U.S. probe done by Jeff Sessions, the recusal of self is another distraction. As Gary Cohn stole the papers from Trump's desk, we all sighed with relief at the thoughts of what could have been. And, if that is what it took to never speak to him again, I'd say there was never any respect to begin with. Claiming that Google rigs the results of our searches, we chuckle uncomfortably realizing that the paranoia is insulting. With all the things in this world to work on, why would the president be googling himself?

I HAD LUNCH WITH A REPUBLICAN YESTERDAY....

on Jun. 1, 2016 at 10:56 AM

Quote Like Reply to Post

Yesterday, I was taking care of a patient's financial assistance, and afterwards I walked him over to the urgent care clinic in the back of the hospital to see the doctor for his issue. During the process we chatted a little, but I mostly listened to what he had to say with a smile while processing him.

On my lunch break, I went outside with a plate of hot wings and macaroni salad from our cafeteria and sat at the picnic

table. My patient saw me eating, and he walked up to me and asked if I mind if he sat with me. I said, of course not, so he sat down at the table with me. He had a bag of chips and a soda from the vending machine and told me that they took good care of him, and that he was waiting for the pharmacy on site to open back up after lunch.

He then said that he was starving, so I offered him some of my chicken wings turning my plate towards him, and we ate off of the same plate together. We chatted about the weather at first, because it was beautiful out with the bluest of skies and fluffy clouds. Then we got on the subject of Hurricanes, and what we both did for

Hurricane Rita, mentioning how we both hoped to not have a bad season this year. We did not have a winter this year, so the summer will be miserable.

And then he mentioned politics, uh oh...lol He said that he was scared of Obama, and that the Obamacare junk frightened him, so he quickly went from Medicare to Humana once he found out that insurance would be mandatory for everyone. He told me that he did not realize that Medicare was an insurance, so fear just overtook him. And, he still has to pay the premium to Medicare, plus now he pays over one hundred bucks a month to Humana for switching. He said how grateful he is to us to have this program to help him, otherwise he would not be able to afford his medicine, and as soon as he can he will switch back to Medicare.

I told him that God does not give us a spirit of fear, and that the fear he felt came from the enemy. He smiled and said, "Sister you are right, God did not call us to fear anything." He asked me if I liked Donald Trump, and I laughed and said I would like him to give up everything he has to the Kingdom of Heaven. He almost choked on his chicken wing...lol

Then I said, I am feeling the Bern, because his image is already on the one-dollar bill. And that was it, he died, laughing that is!!! He said, "I like you, you have an awesome sense of humor," and he left.

October 2016

Everyone take a bended knee, and then Stand for Liberty!! Our leader is the embodiment of the heart of America, the great Nation of debt, greed, lust, hatred, deceit, as the fallen forsaken by division.and self-righteousness we separate. Heeding not the teachings of excellence but succumbing to the views of the world with wicked jealousy. Cold hearts and closed eyes to the Light ever before them, pay close attention and remove the blinders. See, the heart of man will change as minds are enlightened with the truth, and all will know that our differences are what makes us great. Once together as separate entities working for one because there is nothing we can't accomplish. Unlike Congress.

The Great Nation of Babylon is falling, listen and hear the silence from afar. We are in the perfect moment for rising up and overtaking this Nation for God. He will fight the battle, and it is already done. By His Blood we are anointed and will win. Once our government collapses, and we need the help of our neighbors we will come together as One Land not separated by boundaries, borders, nor walls. There is only one way, and it is not the ways of Trump. But Jesus is the way and He unites us all into One Body.

There is no division of the Church, and the State, because you cannot separate members from their own bodies. The Church will rule and will be the governing body after the fall, our bodies are the Temples of God our hands are His craftsmanship. We will build His Kingdom, and the Throne will be built in wait of Our Ruler, the only One who can make this world great again. We are the Church, it is not an organization or a building, but the People. And, these People who are called and Chosen by His name will receive the wealth of the wicked without hesitation.

Therefore, we repent, and turn to Our Father and seek His face in prayer and meditation, and the way is laid out on a golden road that lead to Paradise. We do not trust lying lips, and believe slandering gossips, neither do we idolize flags, or lyrics of songs of man. But, let His praises be continuously on our lips, and we pray at all times ceasing not until the Kingdom comes. Let everyone be on bended knee, better yet take two and while you are down there, remember to pray.

Taking a knee as moved by faith, has no controversy over the flag and the National Anthem if America's allegiance was to God first. As we have Oscar De La Hoya and Kanye West envisioning themselves in the presidential seat, so let me add myself to this dream. For in us are the people together as one, we have the power to overcome the corruptness of the government. We have seen it multiple times a day, constant spirals of hypocrisy, President Trump has shown us who he is, and we believe him. The ridiculousness of ego is not the way of the people, we rebuke and bind up all unrighteousness and wickedness in High Places.

Chapter 9

The Church rules over the state of man

Witnessing the attacks and chemical weapons being activated, we pray without cease because hate cannot be stopped through murder, only love will heal us. Wearing a jacket that states that you do not care while visiting immigrant children imprisoned, shows who your allegiance is to, and it is not Jesus. Feeling like we are going around on the playground in middle school, tweets from the President stating that he has pictures of Mueller and Comey hugging and kissing. Speaking the word of God as commanded, we love all people as ourselves, even if they hate us. Being an enemy of fate, lies blurt out bubbles of hate. Loving our enemies as friends held close, the Kingdom shakes the foundation of this world making it all great. Meghan McCain said it best, "America has no need to be made great again", as she said of her heroic father laying him to rest. As the applause was heard across the country, I pray repentance follows and we all are humbled. The White House raised the flag back where it needed to be, and the chastisement done in love reproved an act of penitence. As the wealth of the wicked is held up for the poor, we await the overflow to pour more. As Trump stood by his controversial response to John McCain's death, remember we are never too big to apologize and admit when we are wrong, it's called humility.

The new election slogan is one like never before, "Vote Republican or I'll be impeached", keeps his base in fear. With the rallies happening like something never seen, we remember the tradition and heritage passed down with the removal of sheets. There is no fear in love, but the haters are disgraced, the tapes of Omarosa were made right under Trumps face. The filth of sin brings disgust to God's nostrils, He regurgitates fence straddlers, and requires that we are hot or cold, no in-between. As the President suggested flipping should be outlawed after being implicated, if only we do on to others as we would have them to do us, maybe no one would flip in the first place. The reality is that this is our lives, and not reality television. We deserve leaders that know right from wrong and are just, not just followers that whisper in secret hoping for damage control. I pray that when this train wreck comes to an end, many survivors stand forever united. We bind up the powers that be and are strong in might as We. People it is time to take a righteous stand against all evil in our land. Even if collision is not a crime, if it's not lined up with truth, we shouldn't waste our time. And, for Giuliani to say that truth is not truth, we know that he did not get that sentence from studying the good book. As Maxine Waters cancelled events due to death threats after President Trumps attacks, we remember that the voice of reason speaks in love and fight back. We have important issues that are lost in insignificant tweets, for example healthcare is something that we all need. If both sides worked together for the advancement of medicine for all Americans the cost could come down, but Republicans and Democrats can't agree and we the people suffer. Congress has no idea what it is like to have to pay for health insurance, yet they are making the rules to play on.

This is the twilight zone, because in Heaven there is no fake man-made problems. Healthcare is all of our responsibility. If there be any sick among us let them be healed according to their faith, in Jesus name. We need to start using our powers that have been invested in us and heal the sick. Let empty hospitals serve as shelters for the homeless, and we take care of each other like family. As George Bush and Michelle Obama passed candy from hand to hand giggling, know that the love of Christ crosses over political parties on earth as in the Kingdom. The love of Christ is greater than any political affiliation, Jesus died and rose again to bring us all together. Let us love each other unconditionally despite our differences.

We are told to supply the needs of the

Saints, and to extend hospitality to strangers.

We are to always do good by sharing what

we have with others, God honors sacrifice. If

we have two coats, then we should give one

away, and we are called to share our food in

the same way. We are told to not ever turn

anyone away who is in need, so give to

everyone who ask knowing that God will

repay us. Those who share with the poor will

be blessed, be gracious in the act of lending

as if to God. As we give it will be given

back, and we will be evaluated the same way

we evaluate others. Great joy comes from

giving to the poor, giving life and rescuing

the troubled. The Righteous consider the

poor, but the wicked give us no regard. The

wealthy should not be highly esteemed, and

neither should anyone trust in their riches.

We trust in the One Living God who longs to

give us our hearts desire. Let the rich do

good works, and willingly distribute and

connect with the poor.

If we want good things to come to us,

we must be fair in business dealings, and

generous for evil to not overcome us.

Because we know that the love of money is

the root for all evil. Let us never forget that

it is more blessed to give than to receive.

Only the Righteous will be remembered, we

do not fear bad news, and trust in God with

confidence. So, let the strong help those who

are weak, according to the Word of God.

Proverbs 11 says that the liberal soul shall be made fat, and whoever gives water will also receive it. We are warned not to withhold food to avoid being cursed, but blessings come to those who give. Those who freely shared their gifts with the poor righteousness endures forever, our Trumpets sound fills the Heavens with honor.

The godly loves to give, but the greedy always want more. We cannot shut our eyes and look away from the poverty in our midst but give, so that we have no lack. Do not hesitate to give, so all things that we set out to do will be blessed.

The Spirit of God produces love, joy,

peace, patience, kindness, goodness,

faithfulness, humility, and self-control, and

we should exhibit all these traits if we are

walking as a Child of God. I pray that we

find compassion for one another, forgiving

each other as we are forgiven in Christ.

Because we are holy and Chosen by God, we

have sympathy for everyone out of love with

gentleness. Even our enemies are blessed

with food and drink, this is how we

overcome evil with good. The bible tells us

to love our enemies and do good deeds by

lending to them without hoping for a

payback. This is how we become Children

of the Most High God with great reward,

because we show kindness to the unthankful

and to the wicked.

The wealthy have been given instructions by Jesus on what is expected of them if they decide to follow Christ and be perfect, "Go, sell all of your possessions and give to the poor in order to have treasure in Heaven. The church is founded on Peter and in the book of Acts, every believer met in one place and shared everything they had with each other. Properties and possessions were sold, and the money was shared with the needy. They worshipped every day and ate supper within their congregation happily. But still, we are not saved by doing good deeds, but by our faith in the Lord Jesus Christ.

I was critical of President Trump in the beginning, but now I understand that we must rebuke with love. In 2015 and 2016, I shared several journal entries online, but now I understand that this presidency was meant to be. This is how I felt in the beginning when he first announced his candidacy…

The trumping of Trump...

on Dec. 8, 2015 at 3:35 PM

Tell me the date when America was great?

Please don't say when Reagan ran the country, because he was likable- having characteristics of a righteous nature. That's like comparing grapes to ape droppings, the smell of decay overpowers the sweetness of the fruit. Crack also emerged as an epidemic that the war on drugs, and the just say no campaign could not contain.

When was the Earth great? When has it even been good as a whole?

The Garden of Eden perhaps...

We would have to go back to the beginning within the creation of it all to get the true answer. Since sin entered the world, there has been turmoil, trouble, and trespasses. No man has the power to do what only God can undo. Jesus conquered the greatest task for mankind, and yet this earth does not reflect the good of His nature as sacrificed from within it. God promised to heal the land, and He only can do this through us. In His word it is written, that if we humble ourselves, and pray and seek His face, turn from our wicked ways, then He will hear from heaven and shall heal the land.

We cannot kill evil spirits by wiping out flesh; it will only transfer over to the next body who allows hate into their being. We are not battling people but spiritual forces. There are only two forces good or evil, love or hate, right or wrong. The only way to stop hate is by loving unconditionally our fellow brothers and sisters while meeting their needs with empathy. Do not forget that God hears the prayers of the Jews and the Gentiles, as well as the Christians and the Muslims. The battle is not ours, but the Lords. Condemnation is not for men to consider and vengeance waits on the wrath of Him that created us all.

We must speak boldly with authority as commanded and shown to us from above, decreeing a thing and it is becoming so. We must step out in faith according to the will of God reversing the order back, correcting all unrighteousness. Good is good and bad is evil, and we can either walk through life with the light or in the dark.

We must choose which side we will walk with; either being with those who are called to bring forth the Kingdom, or with those who are against the plan of God. Being an opposing party and oppressor on all matters that proclaim liberating man to the stance ordained at the start of the world, or with those who are called unto the Kingdom of Glory through righteousness having been promised an eternal life with Christ on Earth as it is in Heaven.

Being more in number than those who do not believe but allowing our voices to be silent due to force from those who do not want to hear the truth is unacceptable. After being told not to pray we surrendered to the threats and forgot that we must continue to pray without cease as David did.

Beware of the wolf in sheep clothing, or should I say the slick fox with the fancy hair swoop. He speaks boldly of himself, coming in a power not from above, but of his own might with a false hope of security. Having charisma and appeal, promising that which man alone cannot accomplish; being puffed up with pride while lacking the peace of Christ in his words of criticism. Having characteristics consistent with the anti-Christ contradicting the teachings of the Savior; instead of taking care of the sick, feeding the hungry, and sheltering the homeless an opposition is broadcasted as fear creating a division in which sharing is shunned.

His children recognize his teachings and will not follow after fraud. We the people being one body with many members, all working together towards the goal of redeeming ourselves back to good standing. There is no lack, and we walk by faith knowing that all of our needs will be granted according to the riches in Heaven as His will be done in the Earth.

Christ said in Matthew 25:

35 For I was hungry and you gave me something to eat, I was thirsty and you gave me something to drink, I was a stranger and you invited me in, 36 I needed clothes and you clothed me, I was sick and you looked after me, I was in prison and you came to visit me. 37 "Then the righteous will answer him, 'Lord, when did we see you hungry and feed you, or thirsty and give you something to drink? 38 When did we see you a stranger and invite you in, or needing clothes and clothe you? 39 When did we see you sick or in prison and go to visit you?' 40 "The King will reply, 'I tell you the truth, whatever you did for one of the least of these brothers of mine, you did for me.'

If you withhold food from the hungry, and drink from the thirsty, lodging for the stranger, clothes for those lacking, healthcare for the sick, visitation for the prisoner, then the true image of the evil one exposes its spirit in you which is operating against the will of God. Know this, He lives and never ceased in existing. He sees and knows all, and His power is in us all who believe and trust in the name of the Lord.

Why is it so hard for a rich man to enter heaven? *Ask Trump*

What if he was offered a blessing of perfection in the eyes of God would he accept?

Jesus said unto him, If thou would be perfect, go, sell that which thou hast, and give to the poor, and thou shalt have treasure in heaven: and come, follow me. Matthew 19:21

President Trump said that if he didn't win the election in 2016, it would have been a waste of time. In response to that statement I shared this post in 2016.

Oct. 6, 2016 at 8:35 PM

Trump is not the Savior of this Nation; all he wants to save is his money in bank(s). Let us pray that he does not make it near the White House, because it would

be a waste of America's time. The first couple of years would be spent with him trying to undo everything President Obama did, including snatching away chemotherapy and insurances from people in the middle of treatments. Meanwhile, nothing will get done as unemployment creeps back up to an all-time high, and gas prices and milk reach five bucks a gallon. At the same time the wealthy will be doing wonderful with their decreased tax rate pocketing millions of dollars extra, and middle class will drop down to poverty level creating recessions and famines throughout America. Discrimination will be accepted as law, and the constitution will become optional. We will lose our allies, and his uneven temper will react harshly out of fear and hatred- making us a target of weakness and ridicule to the rest of the world. Electing him would be a catastrophic disaster for America. His losing will be as a saving grace for the love of humanity, and not a waste of time for those who care about moving ahead instead of going backwards. Trump will be just fine afterwards; he will hire the best tax advisers and figure out how to write off all of his loses on his next audited tax return. We cannot gamble away our future in the CaSINo's of Trump, because we as a people have everything to lose. He would take us for every cent that we have and shrug it off as just business. In response to Trumps

whine, about when he loses this will be a waste of time.

June 18 · 2018

The fulfillment of the law is Love. Without love there will be no law or order. We are commanded to love our neighbors as ourselves, and to treat people the same way we would want to be treated. We are to even love our enemies and meet their needs with food and shelter. Mexico and Canada are our closest neighbors, and both countries deserve the same compassion. Do not be fooled and see the truth as a rising force of correction. There is wickedness in high places, and we must wrestle with the ways of unrighteousness. The root of evil will be cut off, and the wealth of the wicked will spread to hands of the less fortunate. Not all government appointments are ordained by God, some rulers are wolves in sheep's clothing or just blatant wolves seeking to devour. And, as the big, bad wolf sought to eat up little Red Riding Hood, the devil seeks to destroy our children. For, the children are the greatest in the Kingdom of Heaven, because they have the faith to trust and believe in the unseen. Our Administration is an abomination to the will of God, and we need to pray for immediate repentance, and a turn from our evil ways. Jesus said let the children come and hinder them not! Stop the nonsense, Mexico is our closest friend and they have helped America even after being stabbed in the back time and time again. Texas to California is rightfully theirs, and as part of the Chosen being seeds of Abraham, they are entitled to take the land that God gave them. Stolen land has no honor, redemption is coming. #FREETHECHILDREN

The time has come, it is now! We are taking a stand against evil and the powers that be, and we are the status of change that is desired. We have fallen into the twilight zone of dark tunnels that lead to nowhere, the only way out is to be rescued.   There, in the midst of our shame at the lowest, the Lord's hand lifts us up in the presence of Light. The truth shall set us free, and we ponder the word, IMPEACH. We stand united as People over Party! Our affiliations do not contaminate our morals and integrity. The egomania is nauseating, and we need a day without the drama of Trump media spectacles. We know right from wrong, and we are not silent at the misbehaving of our peers, but rebuke and demand correction. Acts of rage, anger, and slander must be avoided, as we speak with purity and not vileness with filthy language erupting from our mouth. Alternative facts seems to have taken us to alternate universe, and the illusion is undeniably deceptive. Non-disclosure agreements and pay-offs for favors, speaks only of the corruption that is made available to us. We know the word, and truly believe that every secret said in the dark will be heard in the daylight, and the whispers inside closed off rooms will be announced from rooftops. Everything hidden will manifest, all concealing will be illuminated. Those who confess and forsake their transgressions will find compassion. We must discern our errors and admit our hidden faults. Let us not be disgraced by the secret things that are talked about. Not participating in the fruitless acts of night, we expose the darkness just like a flick of a light switch. Putting on our armor of light, we see that day approaching, we love God and come close with no fear as evil is exposed. As allied countries plan protest at the hint of President Trumps arrival, and violence threaten the constant rallies, wouldn't it be a good thing to remove the beam out of our own eye before taking the speck out of our neighbors. Fumbling for the proper words to use in appropriate situations, we have heard way too many un-presidential statements. As the Republican party pointed out the cruelty behind the roast of Sarah Huckabee's looks, let them hold Trump accountable for his insults and stop letting him off the hook. Being guided by the spirit at all times, we need to pray before we speak to keep the peace. There is no need to prepare our words when true, because the spirit inside of us will give us righteous utterance and approval. Having an approval rating that is plummeting, it is time to examine the heart and repent. Consequences and sanctions coming for those who broke the law and tampered with our election process, as a result of an anonymous op-ed piece that has our administration on its toes. Hiring the best people reams as false when the rate of turn-over is ridiculously high, if everything was running like a fine oiled machine, why so many lies?

Heavenly Father We come before you humbly with repented hearts. You said in your word that you will heal our land and forgive us of our sins, if we humble ourselves and pray, repent, seek your face, and turn from our wicked ways. We have yet to have this healing, because we have failed to ask you for it, and to do your will.

At this hour, we ask you Father to forgive us of all of our sins, and to let your will be done in this earth. Search the hearts of your children Lord and find a remnant of your love among us. Let us be the Light in this world of darkness that you called us to be. We know that it pleases you to give us your Kingdom on Earth, and that you honor your promises.

You promised us an inheritance Lord, and we rise up to claim our allowance. We pray for those who do not know you or believe in you to have a change of heart, for you told us that all will be changed in a twinkling of an eye at the sound of the trumpet. May the flash of your Light come swiftly without cause, and when the dead put on their new bodies of incorruption may the Angels sing a praise loud enough to fill this entire world with your glory.

Knowing that many of us are called to be Saints, and to march in with great numbers before you Lord, we speak life eternal and we shall live and not die. The word tells us that the Saints will judge the world, and your judgment is upon us.

Your love, grace, mercy, favor, and provision is sufficient enough for us Lord. We need your power, for your will can not be accomplished in the earth by our own might.

We need you to move in this place, this day Lord. You said that you would not stay angry with us long, and you will turn your face back to us. Pour out your spirit upon all flesh Father, let your children dream dreams from your innermost thoughts, and have visions from above to change this earthly place of havoc to a manifestation of your heavenly home of peace, love, and abundant joy.

Looking not at what is currently happening but let us think of what you have in store for us beyond the horizon. You tell us to call those things that are not as though they are, to walk by faith and not by sight, to lean not to our own understandings, and in all of our ways acknowledge you and you shall direct our path. And, Father that is what we are doing, it might look like we are unworthy, but you have made us worthy.

Those who are lost, and do not know you fill them up with your love and let them feel your presence just as you did for me. For every mouth will confess, and every knee will bow before your Son Jesus Christ, and you are just to forgive us of all of our sins. Let us not be tempted, may the path of escape be readily available for us to walk through.

As humans our flesh is wickedly evil, and constantly attacking the spirit you gave us to serve you. We bind up our bodies, as Christ was bonded on the Cross asking for our wills to be obedient to your will for us. And, our desires to be sacrificed as your desires for us produce the fruit of Righteousness.

You have revealed to us that the time for Satan's rule is short, and I say to you that he has had his way in the earth long enough. The destruction he has caused in your people Lord needs to be repaired, we need you to lead us down the correct path. We fear no evil, because we know that you are with us. The comfort and peace you bring is greater than any thought or matter in our lives.

Because of your love for us, you allowed your Son to be crucified for us while we were in our sins, you covered us and kept us blameless before the throne. The beating He endured was for us to receive healing from all sickness and diseases. He suffered, died, and was buried, so that we can have His strength, be liberated, and have eternal life. He rose on the third day not to be empowered in His body, but to give us His power in Our bodies, so that we could do greater things than He did.

Because, He is in us all, we can do all things through Him. It is not our strength, but yours, and it is not our will but yours be done Father. We love you, and we thank you for everything you have done for us, and for what you will continue doing for us. Keep us in your ways, renew your spirit in us daily, remember your promises you made to us.

We honor you; we glorify you, and we keep our minds stayed on you. For you are the Author and the finisher of our faith, and you are working out your perfect salvation in us all. We do not know when your Kingdom will come here, but we hold on to the promises that you made to us and walk by faith knowing that if you said it, it shall come to pass. Not knowing the day or the hour, we know that you are always on time.

This is the day that you gave us, and we rejoice in you and are glad. We choose to serve you this day, and to do the work of building up your Kingdom as you called us to do. We do this, and all things through your Son Christ Jesus. May He reign, rule, and abide in you and in the Heavens and Earth forevermore. Amen and Amen.

Let there be peace in the Earth! Through the lowest valley to the highest mountain, on every Continental surface, over the seas and in the air, let there be peace everywhere. Being created inside the womb then coming out, born-again, changing from within we cast away all doubts. As a people determined to make this world better, we unite as One and turn this hell on earth into Heaven. Standing together hand in hand we face evil head on and come up with a plan. Half the battle is won by knowing the way, having victory comes as we conquer each day. Hate is a force that has a weakness, we kill it with love and practice meekness. Having smothered the fires of evil as flames dying in misty winds, we do deeds of goodwill, and have lives worth living in the end. No more wars, crimes, or any sadness, we make the place of Promise, thy Kingdom Come, BELIEVE IT HAPPENS! We all have one Creator, Our Father the Maker of the earth, moon, sun, and stars, things seen and unheard of are now known, mysteries solved. The love God gave has already overcame the tribulations of this world, and as we denounce the world's views and accept His will, we will have peace on earth. Turning from all ways of wickedness adhering to the laws established, bringing awareness to injustices, revolution to adversities, with healing through forgiveness. Aiming to please God above all others, we ask for peace to be unto us as it is in Heaven. We have no fears and our troubled grievances no longer ache our hearts, instead His peace was left to us, given to never part. For us all a Son was given, the government rest on His shoulders, and the increase of His power will have no end. As the Lord dwells within our hearts, His zeal is upon us, and His love never parts. He will wipe away every tear from our eyes, and no more people will have to die, no pain or even heartbreak, for all former things will pass away. The Faithful and True who judges rightfully and makes war, riding in on a strong white horse. With flaming eyes of fire, wearing a jeweled crown, clothed in a robe dipped in blood, the name that we know Him by is the word. As we follow Christ, dress in our purest whites, we present ourselves as His Army and righteously fight. Striking down the nations with the sword of His mouth, we welcome the iron rod treading the wine press with fierceness and the wrath of God.

Reaching across the lines of effective communication, we plan for increase to benefit the Kingdom. Taking off the blinders, our spiritual eyes are open, we defend ourselves again the big, bad wolf that stands ready to eat us. The wolf will dwell with lamb, and the leopard shall lay with the goat, and the calf and the lion together with a child leading us all. As Martin Luther King's granddaughter Yolanda said, "This should be a gun-free world. Period." We will beat our weapons into plowing instruments, and plant gardens and vineyards in abundance. For our former President Obama to give a speech rebuking Trump, it was a refreshing moment in thirsty times and was right on point.

I realize now that I went about all wrong, and those posts will only drive us farther apart. In order to come together, we must correct in love in order to be heard. We must all be made humble, and hopefully we can work this out on our own, otherwise God will do it for us.

Let us speak with humility and not toot our own horns, for the sound of the horn at judgment will humble us in truth. Trump said, "No administration has accomplished more in the first 90 days than he did. Trump has said on more than one occasion that he alone can save us/and fix this mess, and the crowd went wild...

How many times have members of Trumps own party claimed to be disgusted by something he said or done? Any offenses hinder the prayers of our president and his colleagues. The disinvites, and rebuke was short lived when party came before people.

Let there be forgiveness, and repentance before the offering is made.

Chapter 10

Specializing in the impossible

This is how you end wars....

To live in peace with no wars is easily attainable, and the brilliant people in high places that have yet to make this dream a reality baffle me. As Americans, we have beams in both of our eyes blinding our sight; therefore, we are in no position to go to other countries and tell them how to live in their land. First, we must clean up our own country, transforming every street into a safe haven.

It takes less effort to love and do good than it does to hate and do evil. Whether we believe in God or not, we have the ability to treat each other with respect and kindness. So, though I use these following bible verses to prove my points of peace, I am speaking to all people from my heart with love, believers or not.

Here are the steps to bring forth peace, and to abolish all acts of war in the Earth.

Be gentle and forbearing with one another, if we have a complaint or difference against another, readily pardoning each other, even as the Lord has freely forgiven you, so must you also forgive. Colossians 3:13

Love your enemies, bless them that curse you, do good to them that hate you, and pray for them which despitefully use you, and persecute you. Matthew 5:44

Therefore if your enemy hunger, feed him, if he thirst, give him drink: for in doing so you shall heap coals of fire on his head. Romans 12:20

You see it is really quite simple. Once we move pass the acts of war and love our enemies as ourselves, we can bring forth the Kingdom of peace, love, and happiness forevermore. We will sit down with our enemies offering to meet their needs, and with love we bless them with good. In return they will love us back, and we can then discuss creating the needed mass production of Solar Bubbles, instead of the redundant talk of Nuclear weapons. ☺ ;)

While we are blissfully loving each other with all of this good, let the Matrix inspire us into making virtual reality games for the soldiers to play in the comfort of their living rooms for pay. It will be just like war, only no casualties on either side.

Dec 3, 2009 at 12:31 PM

Oldie by Me.

We are all the same in spirit differing only as ourselves in body, either we are living our lives as we please, or we are living to please God. It is not our ways that are holy, but His way, and in Him our minds and souls are United into One being.

As we all are changed into the image of meekness, and humbled to live peacefully with each other, our minds are renewed with the washing of clean thoughts. It is not our will but His will being done in our lives, and we rejoice in the great work that He is doing in us.

Having good and evil in each of us, we put our thoughts and feelings in subjection to the powers of creation that made us. The Lord created good and evil, the Light and the dark. We either believe that there is a God, there are no gods, or many gods, and some people are unsure either way.

We have nothing or something, we are nobody or somebody, and there is one way or no way. We speak life or death, being positive or negative with the cancellation of all doubt. There is no in-between, we are either hot or cold, and those of us that are comfortable in the warmth of covering up our true face will soon have the wool pulled from over our eyes.

Submitted to the will of God, we are no longer ourselves but His servants who are called by His name for a purpose greater than the world. We are on earth, but not of this world, having in us the Light to overcome all darkness.

Let us come together as One for the sake of Him that gave us the right to everlasting life.

We are all the same in Him who made us in His image. Looking in the mirror we see our outward appearance as a reflected image of ourselves, though the true reflection of who we really are is on the inside. Our hearts are being examined, and within the emotions of brokenness there we will find ugliness or beauty.

Be beautiful today! Love you.

Repent!!

THE KINGDOM IS IN OUR HANDS!!!

Ye are of God, little children, and have overcome them: because greater is he that is in you, than he that is in the world. 1 John 4:4

ABRAHAM LINCOLN SAID THAT GOVERNMENT OF THE PEOPLE, BY THE PEOPLE, AND FOR THE PEOPLE, SHALL NOT PERISH FROM THE EARTH. J.F.K TOLD US NOT TO ASK WHAT OUR COUNTRY CAN DO FOR US BUT ASK WHAT WE CAN DO FOR OUR COUNTRY. AND, THE FAMOUS SAYING THE PRESIDENT OF OUR TIMES IS KNOWN FOR, "GRAB EM BY THE…" CANNOT BE TYPED IN A SPIRITUAL BOOK.

We know that everybody needs to be quick to hear, slow to speak, and slow to anger, because the anger of man does not produce the righteousness of God. We should also add that man should be slow to angrily tweet as well, there is no good coming from such things. We must put away all anger, wrath, malice, slander, and obscenities from our mouths. People who use restraint with their words have knowledge, and those with a cool spirit understand. Telling it like it is and flying off the handle when provoked does not make you smart, but contrary. No corrupt talk should come out of our mouths, instead we build each other up with edification. Our words should grace those who hear, and not hurt. The best way to stay out of trouble is to keep our mouths closed, loud-mouthed boasters only seek to please themselves. To be a good leader we must put others before ourselves. The temperament of the president should quiet arguments and not provoke division. The good and the evil in us is shown when we open our mouths and speak, for our words come from the abundance of our hearts.

We have a president in office that insulted women, the disabled, and many others daily. He makes judgments based on appearance and has been biased towards immigrants. We are to treat others as we want to be treated, so as Melania's parents became citizens others in that circumstance should as well.

I am not saying that Trump can't make it into Heaven, but first he MUST sell all of his possessions and give it to the poor!!

I really need to have a conversation with Trump. Let us pray...

And again, I say unto you, It is easier for a camel to go through the eye of a needle, than for a rich man to enter into the kingdom of God. Matthew 19:24

Let us not contradict the way that Jesus Christ walked.

REPUBLICANS AND DEMOCRATS UNITED!

Republicans and Democrats have no choice but to unite as One Party. The division in the House will cause our Nation to fall! Someone needs to be the adult and agree to disagree, while working to bring forth our visions individually. We being a country indivisible is false, and children can see how ridiculous this has become.

What would it take for us to have no parties, becoming one house of people working for the good of mankind?

Every Kingdom divided against itself is as a wasteland, no city or house divided against itself will stand. Paul made an appeal to us by the name of our Lord Jesus Christ, that we all agree and to not be divided among ourselves. We must unite in the same mind, because we are all called to the same judgment. The only way to end the fighting is

to unite in Christ, because He is not divided.

Many say that Jesus was a socialist, if so, why not embrace

His ideals?

Socialist or just crazy?? Be honest

Posted by

- **<u>Godstar</u>**

on Apr. 2, 2010 at 6:53 PM

<u>Platinum Member</u>

My dream for the world.......

All people will be sheltered in mansions of their design,

fed buffet style, clothed in garments of their

choice, receive water and electricity, and of course have access to health care and all other perks of modern technology at NO COST.

How?!?

Money will no longer be used, and the spirit of volunteerism will engulf all people to acts of charity.

Of course, everything will be regulated, but the day to day stresses of living will no longer be a factor in this life.

Why is this dream a nightmare for so many people?

With love, and through Christ all things are possible.

And who the hell is going to pay for all these goodies you promise?

Trump. And, all of his buddies.

The wealth of the wicked has been held up

for the just. It is hard for a rich man to see

Heaven, les he sale all he has and gives the

money to the poor.

As a woman of God, being an open

vessel for the Spirit to use me, I am sharing

the message that the Lord has given me. The

word is a double-edge sword, and it will

pierce the heart. Many have a heart of stone,

but we pray that God will give us all a heart

of flesh. As the Holy Spirit joined with the

Son and Our Father, being in the Body of

Christ we make One. Risen with Jesus

Christ called forth with the Saints hearing the

Sound of Trumpets!

Hear me now, we must stop sinning, no one who loves Jesus continues to sin.

All things are possible to those that believe, and I believe without any doubt that words live, as seeds taking root producing fruit, so shall we reap every word spoken in abundance at Harvest.

Here is my faith!

As my first landlord Mrs. Ellis would say when she wanted to be nosy.... Tell me something?

Why is it acceptable in some instances (work, ball games, clubs, anywhere almost everywhere) to use profanity and have vulgar banter talk in the presence of those who are unknowingly offended, and yet reading a bible or speaking scripture in public causes an uproar of commotion?

As a 911 Operator almost all personal from the CEO to the janitor, police department, fire, and ambulance had dirty mouths, even I at one point until I changed how used words, so I'm not judging but observing. I realized that words have power, so I am slow to speak unless it is meaningful. At work at 911, I was not allowed to have a bible, but naughty magazines were your business. Needless to say, we (like-minded) get run off from jobs like that... I stayed there 9 months, I was the last to survive of my entire class(6 of us-and the ones with seniority bragged of their high turn around rate). I have had many jobs same story different people, places and outcomes. I have worked at the Library, Phone Company, Dillard's, Hospice Care, Tax Preparer and Medical Field. Admissions department 5 years current. Just sharing a little background...

Nobody cares what the next person is doing unless it is hurting them, so how does it hurt you if I pray in public?

Sure, praying in the closet is great at time when placed, but this generation needs a drastic intervention of saving grace. The

word also says to pray at ALL times, and do
not cease.

Is force fed scripture worse than
overhearing edible pantie talk, or gansta rap
in the park?

How about the President saying it like
it is, can we the people tell the truth instead,
and call it as it should be?

Why does dropping it like it's hot, and
stanky legging it bring rooms of smiles, but
sanctified holy ghost dancing is a joke in this
generation?

The great falling away has happened
as fulfillment of prophecy. Now know this,
the end of this confusion has come.

This is why we must put a girdle on our tongues, be slow to speak and quick to hear.

Why is teaching the bible and reciting prayer in school a problem, is it because it is true and Satan wants to keep us deceived, if not and it is a fairy-tale why not use it as another book for reading comprehension?

Remember, Jesus said let the children COME!

Trump just revealed that aliens are....

Posted by

- **<u>Godstar</u>**

on Mar. 14, 2018 at 3:43 PM

<u>Second Coming</u>

Coming...

I knew it. Lol

He can't hold water...

Pay attention, don't laugh aliens are coming.
But they are my Friends. Military in space
won't stop us.

Trump's Call For A 'Space Force' Makes Him
The Laughingstock Of The Galaxy

President Donald Trump thinks the United
States should launch a "Space Force," a

branch of the military devoted to wars in space.

"Space is a war-fighting domain, just like the land, air and sea," Trump said on Tuesday at the Marine Corps Air Station Miramar. "We may even have a Space Force, develop another one, Space Force. We have the Air Force, we'll have the Space Force."

At first, Trump said he wasn't serious about the notion.

"Then I said, 'What a great idea!' Maybe we'll have to do that,'" Trump said. "So, think of that: Space Force, because we are spending a lot and we have a lot of private money coming in, tremendous."

He also described the U.S. military as "vital

to ensuring America continues to lead the

way into the stars

Chapter 11

Making our World great again

Love, peace, and happiness to all who love the Lord, and

accept His will as their own.

If God is for me, then who can be against me?

For the Pope to call President Donald Trump evil, and to condemn the building of the wall suggesting bridges is offensive. Many priests should be condemned on that level for what they have done to children, and there is a wall around the Vatican. We are not supposed to attack the person, but the evil spirit. And, only the Saints who are covered in the Blood of Christ with corruption can judge this world.

We are not wrestling against a person, but spirits in high places....

narcissist or a sociopath.... those are the words some people used to describe Trump repeatedly throughout his campaign...

Some called him the Anti-Christ, and Obama was called the same. But the Anti-Christ is not one person, it is the spirit of many. Anyone who goes against the teachings of Christ and denies that He lived and rose again is in error and operating under the Anti-Christ spirit.

This appears to be the reason that the people worship the Antichrist, not because of his smooth speech or anything like that, but because he seems to be resurrected from the dead, Obviously Obama has never been killed and come back to life in front of everybody.

I pray that we all walk as God guides us, and that we do not consider our own will. May the Lord's will be done, and not ours. We are the Children of God, and this is the Last Hour. We know that the Anti-Christ has come, it is in the world already, and that time is speeding up to an end. So, do not deny that Christ Jesus is the Son of God, and do not be deceived.

We all have a good side or an evil side, and there is no good on both sides. What we must do is control our flesh and submit our spirits to Christ.

I believe that Donald Trump along with Party and affiliations united against the oppressed has shown Anti-Christ tendencies, therefore I pray for him to come into the full knowledge of Christ. I do not stroke the cords of Hillary's harp likewise, as the wise proverb says, "different wing same bird". I am waiting on the reign of Jesus Christ.

Momafortune 2016

Those who have ears to hear, hear in Spirit the truth!

The book of Daniel describes the Antichrist in chapter 11, take a look.

Instead of wonder, research. Wisdom is available to all who ask of the Lord, and knowledge is power. God bless.

The devil comes to kill, steal, and destroy and seeks to ravish us like a roaring lion. But, know this, as the devil name is flipped, he ceases to exist, (lived-devil in reverse), the end to evil is near we win with the victory of Christ. LOVE.

Our President threatened to turn back the migrant caravan, but we needed to call on Calvary. I sense the spirit of the murdered

Indians of North America as reincarnated souls of entitlement. Let us pray for the will of God to be done. I was taught this in 5th grade in the 80's, we knew then that the day would come...be on team Abraham and reap the blessings. A child will lead us!

Light is ever before you, and the darkness is exposed. It's simple, whatever happens in the dark will come to light. Those hidden things will be exposed, it is biblical. Those who are being slandered, if there is no truth to it, have nothing to worry about. We don't walk in fear, but in power and soundness. The truth will set us free, there is nothing scary in Christ.

Now, I speak to Satan and all of his angels...

RUN SATAN, YOU DIRTY EVIL NO GOOD DECEIVER, FLEE IN THE NAME OF JESUS!!!

For you know that your time is short, and we have already defeated you. You have lived in the earth long enough, and I come to cast you out of every dark crevasse you have infected with your murderous, deceitful, thievish ways of immoral acts of lusts and hateful envy. You are legion being many, but we are many members of one union set to destroy you and your works. Your touch on my children come with the ramifications of my hands knocking you out into the sea of forgetfulness in which you came, and once you fall threw, and land back into your pit of volcanic fire, forever will you be locked up, and we won't let you out.

Singing in harmony of the Lord's power, glory, victory, majesty and greatness, every voice in heaven and in the earth, Rejoice. Thy Kingdom has Come, Oh Lord, we exalt your Name above all, as the earth's and Heaven's Head. The Loud voice in Heaven shouts, Now has come salvation, and strength, and the kingdom of our God, and the power of his Christ: for the accuser of our brethren is cast down, which accused them before our God day and night. And they overcame him by the blood of the Lamb, and by the word of their testimony; and they loved not their lives unto the death. Therefore rejoice, ye heavens, and ye that dwell in them.

Woe to the inhabiters of the earth and of the sea! For the devil is come down unto you, having great wrath, because he knoweth that he hath but a short time. Revelation 12:10-12

I am not being silent anymore, for I know the power that lives on the inside of me. I will shout from the Mountaintops and shake the foundation of the earth, as I declare His Kingdom for the Namesake of Our Father.

THIS IS OUR WORLD!!! We who are in Christ Jesus have Authority. You have had your run Satan for too long, and the destruction is atrocious. Let be it done, as a promise to the descendants of Abraham, from every nation, creed, denomination, and none we come together as one body in Christ Jesus, be ye changed in a twinkling of an eye, let us walk

in our true identity as Saints. In our hands is

the healing for this whole world, and in our

mouths are words of restoration and

correction. May the crooked paths be made

straight, and narrow is the gate.

LINE UP!!!!

Get straight, it is time to get right.

Stand tall, and do not fall, we are about to battle.

Not with swords, guns, and fists, but with words. For we

have the ability to give life or take it away

with the words we say. WAKE UP, no more

sleeping open your spiritual eyes and see, it

is Me. Not the one who types in body, but

the spirit of the Most High in embodiment.

Amen. Repent!!! THE KINGDOM IS AT HAND!

May this book wash your eyes out after Stormy's book and unite this nation .

The reality is that this is our lives, and not television. We deserve leaders that know what's right and are just, and not followers that whisper in secret when something is terribly wrong.

The same God over the Jews is over the Gentiles, the same as the Christians and the Muslims. The sign that people look for in the Coming of Christ is upon you, and the blinders on your eyes shall fall off as the twinkling takes effect. We are many, but One with differences that make us great in Him. There are no religions, or denominations in Heaven, only the Chosen and the Called. Hear today, through the Spirit that works in us, and know that we are blessed to have an invitation of grace extended. In love there is nothing that we cannot accomplish, and together we will create the Kingdom of Heaven on earth. Keep your eyes on the sky, and know that I speak the truth only, NEVER LIES!

Our provider is the Creator of ALL, and His law of love is above the lawlessness of man. Whatever good thing we ask for in His Name will be given to us according to the riches and glories in Heaven, let no man boast that he gave when all things are from God.

We do not seek scandal, but those of us who seek the Lord reveal the evil hidden in dark places!

Do not be petty, we the people are powerful. God is great, and greater is He that is in us than he that is in the world.

Crossing party lines, sharing candy from republican to democrat, that's how the Body of Christ looks, all people in love.

They been waiting for a race war, and it will have a unifying effect by every person who loves. The victory belongs to Jesus, the End! Hallelujah, Amen. The enemy loses, we WIN.

We are being tested by God, the righteous and the wicked, who is on the Lord's side? The one who loves violence, the soul of God hates. Humbling ourselves we apologize and admit being wrong, there is nothing wrong with humility. Jesus is the perfect example.

We are witnessing a turnover in office at an unexplainable rate, resignations and firings left and right, to make light let us sings, Another one bites the dust... the end of this world is at Hand.

Chastisement done in love as reproved an act of repentance henceforth!

Man has failed, but the victory belongs to Jesus! We win eternally through faith in Christ and walk by faith and not by sight. Do not cause little children to suffer, there is no reward in the Kingdom for such evil.

We must not forget where our loyalty should be, and that is with God let no man deceive.

There is no fear in love, only haters should be terrified. Too many times fear is played upon, and we cancel out our faith. Let us remember that we have been given power to do all things in Christ Jesus and will not be afraid.

We know that a good man brings forth good things out of the good stored up in his heart, and an evil man brings evil things out of the evil stored up in his heart. And, the mouth speaks what the heart is full of.

We do not say racially insensitive things, call names or tear down, we restrict ourselves as the tongue has a girdle on it from now on. When people are lowdown and dirty to us, we are to keep it clean and soar above them.

Setting the atmosphere according to the peace of Christ in our world which is this entire earth. The drama will leave, nobody has time for it in the Kingdom. Get right or be left behind. In Jesus Name, Amen.

We are not to be ugly and destroy stars on the Walk of Fame, but repair the broken, uplifting the lost, and most of all we must pray.

I giggle at the thought of Space Force, can't help the thought. The Aliens are coming in 2020. The movie was prophetic...lol

If the wall is built one act of nature could blow it down as the wind, safety will come from having God within.

There's not enough cyberspace to keep up, daily news feeds blowing up. Russian spies caught working after ten years in Moscow US embassy, good grief.

Evil is a divided country with no love for the least. Remember Jesus is undercover in the least of us and all who believe. I speak the truth in love, and some people can't handle it. I'm Anti-Satan and the Light in me exposes the enemy. We win! Victoriously.

Let the Church say, Amen. The time to come forward proclaiming the truth to the world is upon us. We must preach the gospel of Christ to everyone before the end comes. The church cannot be separated from the body of Christ, because we are One people in Him.

Our bodies are the Church, and the temple within us holds the spirit of Christ. Greater is He that lives in us than he that is in the world. Instead of the Religious Liberty Task Force declaring a holy war on people, let us remember it is not flesh we are battling, but demons.

I pray that when this Train wreck comes to an end, many survivors stand together forever united. We bind up the powers that be and are strong in might as We! People it's time, let us be united. Collusion might not be a crime, but even the devil knows that it isn't right.

President Trump's attorney, Rudy Giuliani actually stated with a straight face that, "Truth isn't truth", and we know that the word says that Jesus is the way, the truth, and the life. No one comes to the Father except through Him, and we who are called know the truth, and the truth will set us free. We are to show love through actions and truth, not words and speech. Our words must be true, and people will be sanctified by the truth. Do not believe the lies of Satan, and always recognize the voice of reason and truth. Those who believe in God and worship in spirit must abide in His Spirit and truth at all times.

The voice of reason speaks with love, we do not attack people physically or with words. And, death threats due to opposing views is absurd and should be unheard of. This whole administration and entire world needs to repent, and act like we are sorry.

As many lives were lost illegally crossing the border for a dream, let us pray that we can find a way to help our neighbors and meet their needs. May the intercessions and petitions on behalf of love ones, and those loved, and love be accepted and manifested in the earth for Kingdom purposes. May we be at peace and rest peacefully in the bosom of Christ, always and forever.

Some are not able to reach across the lines of effective communication, and they have no plans for anything that does not benefit their own pockets. But God laughs at the plans of man.

As those babies crying out for their mothers and fathers at the border, we cry out to Our Father in Heaven, saying Abba. Please show us grace and mercy. We are commanded to love ALL people even our Hispanic neighbors! Our will does not outweigh God's plan. Isaiah 61 is our instructions.

I speak the word of God as He commands me, and love ALL people as myself, even if they hate me. Do not be the enemy of fate, love God and do not discriminate. Have no enemies, but only friends who are held close. The Kingdom of Heaven will make the earth great again, no man has that power without faith.

Any policy or law that causes separations of families should be banned; it is not of God but the devil. God blesses all of the families of the earth

Can we get metal detectors in the schools please? If we can prevent shootings at airports we certainly can do better at schools.

As a woman we should think greater of ourselves than what man thinks of us. Being created above and not beneath, we have in us the power to bring down Heaven. Not our will be done, but Christ Jesus.

As President Trump mourned young beautiful lives destroyed by the Russian Probe, we grieve the loss of lives tragically taken in our hometowns. He never pretended to be a Sheep, but openly admitted his wolfism. Let the blinders come off and see the truth, he loves Russia more than America.

There you see it MAGA hats and swimwear, multiple times a day in constant spirals of hypocrisy. He has shown us who he is, and we believe it. The ridiculousness of ego is not the way of the people, we rebuke and bind up all unrighteousness and wickedness in High Places. The time is Now! Take a stand against evil and the powers that be and become the status of change.

Chapter 12

Ending with a New Beginning

"I revealed myself to those who did not ask

for me;

I was found by those who did not seek me.

To a nation that did not call on my name,

I said, 'Here am I, here am I.'

[2] All day long I have held out my hands

to an obstinate people,

who walk in ways not good,

pursuing their own imaginations—

[3] a people who continually provoke me

to my very face,

offering sacrifices in gardens

and burning incense on altars of brick;

[4] who sit among the graves

and spend their nights keeping secret vigil;

who eat the flesh of pigs,

and whose pots hold broth of impure meat;

5 who say, 'Keep away; don't come near me,

for I am too sacred for you!'

Such people are smoke in my nostrils,

a fire that keeps burning all day.

6 "See, it stands written before me:

I will not keep silent but will pay back in

full;

I will pay it back into their laps—

7 both your sins and the sins of your

ancestors,"

says the LORD.

"Because they burned sacrifices on the

mountains

and defied me on the hills,

I will measure into their laps

the full payment for their former deeds.”

[8] This is what the LORD says:

"As when juice is still found in a cluster of

grapes

and people say, 'Don't destroy it,

there is still a blessing in it,'

so will I do in behalf of my servants;

I will not destroy them all.

[9] I will bring forth descendants from Jacob,

and from Judah those who will possess my

mountains;

my chosen people will inherit them,

and there will my servants live.

[10] Sharon will become a pasture for flocks,

and the Valley of Achor a resting place for

herds,

for my people who seek me.

[11] "But as for you who forsake the LORD

and forget my holy mountain,

who spread a table for Fortune

and fill bowls of mixed wine for Destiny,

[12] I will destine you for the sword,

and all of you will fall in the slaughter;

for I called but you did not answer,

I spoke but you did not listen.

You did evil in my sight

and chose what displeases me."

[13] Therefore this is what the Sovereign LORD

says:

"My servants will eat,

    but you will go hungry;

my servants will drink,

    but you will go thirsty;

my servants will rejoice,

    but you will be put to shame.

[14] My servants will sing out of the joy of their

hearts,

but you will cry out

    from anguish of heart

    and wail in brokenness of spirit.

[15] You will leave your name

    for my chosen ones to use in their curses;

the Sovereign LORD will put you to death,

    but to his servants he will give another

name.

[16] Whoever invokes a blessing in the land

will do so by the one true God;

whoever takes an oath in the land

will swear by the one true God.

For the past troubles will be forgotten

and hidden from my eyes.

New Heavens and a New Earth

[17] "See, I will create

new heavens and a new earth.

The former things will not be remembered,

nor will they come to mind.

[18] But be glad and rejoice forever

in what I will create,

for I will create Jerusalem to be a delight

and its people a joy.

[19] I will rejoice over Jerusalem

and take delight in my people;

the sound of weeping and of crying

    will be heard in it no more.

[20] "Never again will there be in it

    an infant who lives but a few days,

    or an old man who does not live out his

years;

the one who dies at a hundred

    will be thought a mere child;

the one who fails to reach[a] a hundred

    will be considered accursed.

[21] They will build houses and dwell in them;

    they will plant vineyards and eat their

fruit.

[22] No longer will they build houses and

others live in them,

    or plant and others eat.

For as the days of a tree,

so will be the days of my people;

my chosen ones will long enjoy

the work of their hands.

23 They will not labor in vain,

nor will they bear children doomed to

misfortune;

for they will be a people blessed by the

LORD,

they and their descendants with them.

24 Before they call I will answer;

while they are still speaking I will hear.

25 The wolf and the lamb will feed together,

and the lion will eat straw like the ox,

and dust will be the serpent's food.

They will neither harm nor destroy

on all my holy mountain,"

says the LORD.

Isaiah 65

END OF THE WORLD…

We can see clearly that....

The end of our world is near, what we once loved and held

dear is slipping away never to be seen again.

We can't stop it, the pain pounds hearts like panic, never will

things be the same, the fear of creating

something new seems lame.

Oh, the wretched and the worn are back alone dreading the

day that is coming our way.

The dark shadows of connections lost forever as the wind,

realizing that we are as vapors melting away

into the light.

Venturing into the unknowns with a love that comes with

mourning, we are strong and look forward

without regrets or worries.

Having time to remember, appreciate, and reach out, we embrace as Family forever one with each other.

It could have been worse; we could have had no notification of the end and been left suffering and sick without time to find our friends.

God is good.

We win!!!

Every single island on this planet now, will drop to the oceans floor beneath the ground.

Also, every mountain up high will drop down low, and there will be no more grass to mow.

Places in and around North America will sink below the earth, sweltering with heat they melt away.

All over this world will be the gnashing of teeth, and hollering wails of grief.

It is so, because before it gets better it will get worse.

IT IS WRITTEN! AND, SHALL BE DONE.

Now, you have been warned, and heard the message, LET

EVERYBODY COME!!

From the North, South, East, and West, from every high end

to every pole, off the mountains out of the sea,

you are called as a living soul.

Gather up, and watch the sky, I promise you

this, YOU WILL NOT BELIEVE YOUR

EYES!

The twinkling happens as the sky folds back,

and NONE of us will ever look back.

We are the called and the Chosen, and in the

New Jerusalem we have only one purpose.

Saying here we are the, seeds of Abraham

claiming our heritage, standing in the

Paradise promised.

And every island fled away, and the mountains were not found.

Revelation 16:2

Looking to the skies for signs in the sun, moon and stars, as the seas rumble in agony, nations are confused by the trials of this world. While the powers of heaven are shaken down into the earth, the people faint with fear. Therefore, we keep our eyes open and alert, being fully awake knowing that we do not know the day or the hour that the Lord is coming, we live each day as if He is coming today. As the thief comes at night without the master knowing, so will Christ. For no violation to be found, let us stay awake and not be asleep at the hour break-in.

For the wrath of God is revealed from heaven against all ungodliness and unrighteousness of men, who by their unrighteousness suppress the truth.

The ruler of this world is coming. He has no claim on me, Concerning judgment, because the ruler of this world is judged. We have something that we are sure of, the prophetic word, and we will do well to pay close attention as it is a lamp shining in darkness, the day dawns and the morning star rises in your hearts. We have a thorn placed in our flesh to keep us from being conceited, the revelation of God's Word surpasses greatness.

As we are subjects of the governing bodies that be, there is no authority above God. We do good for the sake of our conscience, to find approval through the grace of God. The time for the offspring of God to come into the promise made in the beginning is here. Let us offer supplications, prayers, intercessions, and thanksgiving for all people, and rulers so that we may lead a peaceful and quiet life, godly and dignified in every way. This is what pleases Our Father, it is good in His sight, because He desires all people to be saved and to come to the knowledge of the truth. There is only One God, and one mediator between God and men, the One- and Only-man Jesus Christ. The God of peace will soon crush Satan under foot, with the weapons of righteousness for the right and the left with truthful speech and the power of God. The god of this world blinded the minds of unbelievers to keep them from seeing the light of the gospel of the glory of Christ, who is the image of God. We are not ignorant of the devil's design, so we will not be outwitted by Satan. Though the serpent deceived Eve cunningly, our thoughts will not be led astray as we are sincerely devoted to Christ. Every argument and lofty opinion raised against the knowledge of God destroyed, and all thoughts held captive to obey the Lord. We present ourselves to God as one approved, a servant with no shame, handling the word of truth with honor. We no longer walk in sin, and do not follow the ways of the world.

Encouraging each other, knit together in love, reaching the full assurance of understanding and knowledge of God's mystery which is Christ, in whom are hidden all the treasures of wisdom and knowledge, we are not deluded with unbelievable arguments.

Since we received Christ Jesus as Our Lord, we walk in Him, rooted and built up in Him, established in the faith, as we were taught, with an abundance of thankfulness. We are filled in Him; Christ is the Head of all with authority. Denying the body, by the circumcision of Christ, having been buried with Him in baptism, raised with Him through faith in the power of God, made alive together with Him, being forgiven of all of our sins, canceling the record of wrongs that stood against us legally. Through the nailing on the Cross, these things were set aside, disarming the rulers and those in authority, putting them to shame through a triumphant victory over the enemy. Being strong in the Lord, in the strength of His might, we put on the whole armor of God, so that we may withstand the schemes of the devil. We are not battling people but flesh and blood, against the rulers, against the authorities, against the cosmic powers over this present darkness, against the spiritual forces of evil in the heavenly places. Taking up the whole armor of God, so that we will be able to stand in the evil day, and having done all, to stand firm. Stand therefore, having fastened on the belt of truth, and having put on the breastplate of righteousness, and as shoes for our feet, having put on the readiness given by the gospel of peace. In all circumstances taking up the shield of faith, with which you can extinguish all the flaming darts of the evil one; taking the helmet of salvation, and the sword of the Spirit, which is the word of God, praying at all times in the Spirit, with all prayers and supplications. To that end, keeping alert with all perseverance, making supplications for all the saints.

Now, may our God and Father Himself, and our Lord Jesus, direct our ways, and may the Lord make us increase and abound in love for one another and for all, as we do for all, so that He may establish our hearts blameless in holiness before Our God and Father, at the Coming of our Lord Jesus with all of His Saints.

Being a Chosen Race, a royal priesthood, a holy nation, a people for his own possession, that we may proclaim the excellencies of Him who called us out of darkness into His marvelous light. Before we were not a people, but now we are God's people; once we had not received mercy, but now we have received mercy. Hallelujah, praise God! Amen.

We have come to life, and will reign with Christ, for a thousand years. After which the rest of the dead will not come to life until the thousand years are finished. This is the first resurrection. Blessed and holy is the one who shares in the first resurrection! Over such the second death has no power, but we will be priests of God and of Christ, and we will reign with Him for a thousand years. Selah.

We have returned rejoicing, saying, "Lord, even the demons are subject to us in your Name". As Satan fell from Heaven like lightning, we have been given authority to tread on serpents and scorpions, and over all the power of the enemy, and nothing can hurt us. But we do not rejoice in this, that the spirits are subject to us, instead we rejoice because Our Names are Written in Heaven. None of us are judged by the Father, but all judgment has been given to the Son. Therefore, we are not ashamed of the Gospel, for it is the power of God for salvation to everyone who believes, to the Jew and also the Greek as well as Christians and Muslims. We are all God's Children, the Seed of Abraham, the line of Isaac and Ishmael, living of the flesh and of the spirit, submitting to God's will. As He breathes on us, His Spirits pours out as oil anointing our bodies in unification with the Son. The Trinity in One, our minds, hearts, and souls in Christ. Conformed into the image of perfect love. This is the adulterous and sinful generation Christ warned us of, and we are not counted among those who are ashamed of the Gospel. We know that this is the Hour, and He comes with the glory of God and the holy angels. The Trumpet is Sounding on the seventh blow!

The Curtains of Heaven are slowing dropping down, and the role as earth pulls the plug. We have all been found in the state of those in the times of Noah, and through compassion take the option. Being forgiven and redeemed it's the Coming of Heaven's Marriage Party. Clean up, and accept the invitation, Christ is at the door of your heart, KNOCKING.

Captive in the presence of God, giving testimony humbly, joined in the sufferings of Christ for the gospel according to the power of God, we have no shame. We know God, and our deeds will rise up to meet the expectations of perfection through the Spirit of Christ working in us. With obedience we accept Christ and do good deeds. Submitting to God, resisting all temptations we watch evil leave, the devil flees. The battle is now within of ourselves, as overcomers we destroy the Me's for, we.   Binding our tongues, no corruption flows from our tongues. We speak of only good reports, and on things that build us up as it fits the time, bringing grace to those who hear. Without grumbling or question we do all things according to the will of the One who sent us here, with only the purpose of Heaven's Kingdom and God's intentions.

As His Children, we are from God and have overcome every evil of this world, Because greater is He that is in us, than he that is in the world.

The Lord shows His compassion for Jacob and chooses Israel, setting us in our own land, foreigners will join us, attaching themselves to the house of Jacob. No longer are we slaves, and our sins of being Masters, are before the graves. Time for reconciliation. We all have sinned and fell short of glory, but now we repent, turn from our wickedness and pray. God is about to bless us and heal our land. This is not something for man. All glory and honor to Him who created us, and all of the Heavens and earths. The Oppressor ceases to exist in the New World awakening, the Lord has broken the staff of the wicked, the scepter of rulers. Now that the Saints have come down to the earth, ignited in the Fire of the Holy Ghost, no one covered by the blood will be cut down. The realm of the Dead below us is all stirring, ready to meet Christ at His Coming. The aroused spirits of the departed are ready to greet Him, every leader in the world rise up from the seats and stand on feet. All the Kings of every Nation give response, notice that we are weak and merely in the spirit overcoming flesh as all are. But who can stand against God? His Hand is stretched out, and no one can turn it back. The First heaven and earth is taking its last breath, passing away before our eyes. And, as life leaves out, the birth of a great surprise comes about, the circle of life as some call it. The New Heaven and New Earth, the Holy City, New Jerusalem, coming down out of Heaven from God, prepared as a Bride adorned for her Husband. The voice from the Throne saying, "Behold, the dwelling place of God is with man. He will dwell with them, and they will be his people, and God himself will be with them as their God. He will wipe away every tear from their eyes, and death shall be no more, neither shall there be mourning, nor crying, nor pain anymore, for the former things have passed away." "Behold, I am making all things new." The peace of Christ rules our hearts calling us into One Body, and we are thankful.

Chapter 13

The Reign of Heaven's Kingdom

As the tugging of heart strings hears soundness, we open our minds to serving oneness. Having only one master, we love God over the world and not money. Being aligned with spirit over flesh, our desires are the Kingdom before earthly possessions and riches. Knowing the rich are destined for misery, the cries and mourning howl in the night when all things pass away. Clothes and gourmet meals matter not, but the naked and hungry, as the widows and orphans who are without. To those much is given, much more is required. Because it is the Last Days, let no treasures be kept away. Putting off self-indulgence and luxury, we have purged our hearts in wait for judgment. Expecting to enter the Kingdom of God, we let go of it all to fit through the camel's eye. Keeping our lives free from the love of money, we are satisfied with love, and have joy abundantly. Gladly giving to the needy, we take all wealth and distribute it freely. To have a treasure waiting in Heaven, we offer up everything we have on earth through living. Eradicating evil by the root, the love of money cravings turns stomachs like spoiled fruit. Gracing the poor with generosity is a loan to God with entitled payment. Those who wish to be perfect must be willing to sell every possession and give the proceeds to the poor. As we come into the perfect knowledge of Christ, we follow His example as the way of direction into Heaven. The rich are obligated to do good things for the poor, be ready to share, and store up a treasure beyond this world. Let those who are strong help the weak, and never forget that it is better to give than it is to receive. It is by the grace of Jesus that even though He is rich for us He became poor, so that by His poverty we might become rich. Those of us who are poor are blessed with the kingdom of God, we are chosen to be rich in faith and heirs of the Kingdom. We who love the Lord receive His promises, and all the good words spoken by God will be fulfilled in us. God is honored by our generosity to the needy, and we do not insult the Lord through oppression. Every heart must decide to give cheerfully, because this pleases our Father. We will be called up together to meet our Maker, the rich and the poor stand at the judgment as favor is granted. The poor, crippled, lame, and blind are the guest of honor at the feast, and repayment comes at the resurrection of the just. At the coming of Christ, on the throne on glory with His host of Angels all Nations will gather, and the people will be separated by the great Shepard. The sheep on His right, and the goats on the left. As the Sheep, we are welcomed and blessed by our Father, inheriting the Kingdom that was prepared for us at the foundation of the world. We welcomed the stranger, fed the hungry, and gave a drink to the thirsty. Providing shelter from the storms of life, and shade from the heat we supported the poor in times of distress. Nothing in this world is worth gaining at the cost of losing our souls, and we do not know the day or the hour that the Lord will come. Therefore, we do not sleep, but we are alert and watchful. As the Saints we love our neighbors, and the Lord blesses us for caring for the poor. As the glory of the Lord rest on us, we show no partiality through faithful acts of our charity for all of those in lack. The wrath of God waits on the repentance of the wicked, and the cost of deliverance has been paid through the blood of Christ. There is no other way around it, Jesus is the only way to the Kingdom, and we must accept His way to be accepted by God. The separation of good and evil is a spiritual battle that we conquer from within, and the Lord is working in us and through us to accomplish His perfect will for our lives. As we persevere into complete matureness, we have no lack, and as we are found blameless let us ask God to generously bestow on us His wisdom. This we know for sure, the sexually immoral and the unjust, those who covet and idolize have no inheritance in the kingdom of Christ and God. We aspire to live in the Kingdom of Heaven always, and we follow the law of love Christ gave to us which supersedes that laws of man and his authority. We once lived in sin and was not joined in the Body of grace. But, through the washing of the word our spiritual ears hear the truth, and we are no longer in the dark. The Light has transformed the deception of this world into the revelation of evil resistance, and through love the repentance of hearts changes the thoughts of men. The only debt that we owe to one another is to love, and through love the law is fulfilled. We surrender our lives for the life of Christ, and not our will be done but only the will of God. In losing our life for the sake of the gospel, we gain eternal life in Christ. There is no waiting on tomorrow, or for the world to change. We accept His will for us today and live every day after for Him. In all our ways we acknowledge Him, and we allow Him to make our path straight. There is no turning to the left or the right, we turn completely away from evil. It is time to make ready the way of the Lord, smoothing out the rough areas for His spirit to flow through. We set to establish the house of the Lord as the chief of the mountain, because this is the last days. Every nation will run as a stream through the hills, and no one will be able to count the tribes of people standing before the throne of the Lamb.

INVITATION TO THE THIRSTY

55 "Come, all you who are thirsty,

>**come to the waters;**

and you who have no money,

>**come, buy and eat!**

Come, buy wine and milk

>**without money and without cost.**

2 Why spend money on what is not bread,

and your labor on what does not
satisfy?
Listen, listen to me, and eat what is good,
  and you will delight in the richest of
fare.
3 Give ear and come to me;
  listen, that you may live.
I will make an everlasting covenant with you,
  my faithful love promised to David.
4 See, I have made him a witness to the
peoples,
  a ruler and commander of the peoples.
5 Surely you will summon nations you know
not,
  and nations you do not know will come
running to you,
because of the LORD your God,

the Holy One of Israel,

for he has endowed you with splendor."

6 Seek the LORD while he may be found;

call on him while he is near.

7 Let the wicked forsake their ways

and the unrighteous their thoughts.

Let them turn to the LORD, and he will have

mercy on them,

and to our God, for he will freely pardon.

8 "For my thoughts are not your thoughts,

neither are your ways my ways,"

declares the LORD.

9 "As the heavens are higher than the earth,

so are my ways higher than your ways

and my thoughts than your thoughts.

10 As the rain and the snow

come down from heaven,

and do not return to it

without watering the earth

and making it bud and flourish,

so that it yields seed for the sower and

bread for the eater,

11 so is my word that goes out from my

mouth:

It will not return to me empty,

but will accomplish what I desire

and achieve the purpose for which I sent it.

12 You will go out in joy

and be led forth in peace;

the mountains and hills

will burst into song before you,

and all the trees of the field

will clap their hands.

13 Instead of the thorn bush will grow the

juniper,

and instead of briers the myrtle will grow.

This will be for the LORD's renown,

for an everlasting sign,

that will endure forever." Isaiah 55

It is hard for us to accept, because His will is not our will. However, His will be done. It will not be easy for the wealthy to accept, but the poor will embrace the blessings due to them from the Father. It will be done as such as it is in Heaven, on Earth in this due season.

Good men leave behind inheritances to their children, but the wealth of the wicked is held up for the Righteous. Blessed are the poor in spirit, for Our Kingdom is in Heaven.

As we the people come together and learn the ways of Christ, we walk in His path. Bringing the law forth through the living word, we stand in judgment with Christ. Whatever He decides it is, and we will beat our weapons into plowing instruments. All nations commit to never attacking another, and never again will war be taught. The Garden of Eden will be born again through our planting, and we will forever live in peace together. The entire government of the world being rest on the Shoulders of Christ, and under the Wonderful, Mighty, Eternal Counselor we will have peace without end.

With His zeal upon our heads, we will accomplish this justly through righteousness. In wisdom and in understanding, fearing the Lord no judgment is made through the eyes or ears. The afflicted and the poor receive the reward of fairness, and the breath of His lips slay the wicked. Our children will not die as infants, and our elders will live out every one of their days. The young will live to be one hundred, and those cursed will not live that long. We will build houses for all people to be sheltered and enjoy eating the fruits that we harvest. Without being removed we live in the houses we build and eat what we plant. Our lifetime will be as a tree, and our hands create the Kingdom. Being blessed by the Lord, there is no calamity and no labor is vain.

Before we call, God answers us, and while speaking He hears us. There will be no evil or pain in all His Holy Mountain. Dwelling in safety we rest and abide under His salvation in the righteousness of God. With trembling we bow down to the Lord reversing in His goodness in the End. Come forth sons of Israel and seek the truth, return to the Lord our God. In gladness we rejoice in His presence after waiting in preparation for this day. He rose up for us with all power, and He hands us the power to do all things in Him. Restoration is bestowed to the Children of God as our fortunes are taken back from the enemy. The day of the Lord is here, destruction comes from the wrath of His Hand. With melting hearts and limpness hands we bear through like a woman in labor, until desolate lands produce fruits. Punishment will be relinquished to the wicked caught in their sins, and every evil will cease at judgment. As the stars of heaven and the constellations dim their light, the sun rises darkened, and the moon cannot be found, all of the arrogant and prideful are wiped out of existence. Immortality replaces the mortal man, as the Lord speaks before His Army. We are the greatness that makes the world great, for we carry out His word in strength of numbers. We endure only in Him, and live as if the time has come, because we do not know the day or the hour. Looking to the skies for wonders and the world for signs, we long for the great and glorious day of the reign of Jesus.

Before the foundation of this world we were called with Him, and in these lasts days His words live through us, keeping us from perishing. With the blood of the precious Lamb, without spot or blemish, we are washed by the word, by His Blood. We are redeemed from the past and are heirs of Christ entitled to take our inheritance promised from the beginning. As we call on the name of Jesus, we are saved. The fullness of the time is now, because the Kingdom of God is in our hands, believe in the gospel, and repent! As the Kingdom of God comes, demons flee by His Spirit. We have been sent to preach the Kingdom of God to every city until everyone has heard the good news. There is nothing more positive than the news of Christ, and His purpose for each of us. It is simply to love and rebuke hate. This is the favorable year of the Lord, His spirit is falling on all His Sons and Daughters, ALL flesh. Greater is He that is in us, and we are proclaiming release for everyone imprisoned, recovery of sight to the blind, setting free the oppressed, as we preach under the anointing. Know now that this scripture is fulfilled, as the blinders come off and we see the truth. Those who are broken-hearted are who matters to Jesus, and we who are in Christ look after the afflicted. For we know the vengeance that the Lord brings to those who refused the least of His people. In bringing the gospel, the miracles flow and the lame walk and the mute talk. In His Spirit we prophesize, share our visions, and dream dreams with Kingdom delivery. Having the Spirit of Christ in us we walk in His statues carefully obeying the commandments. God speaks to us the same as He spoke to Abraham, through the Christ in us He speaks to our transformation. Our eyes are blessed as we can see the goodness of God, and our ears likewise as we hear the truth.

God, after He spoke long ago to the fathers in the prophets in many portions and in many ways, in these last days has spoken to us through His Son, whom He appointed heir of all things, through whom also He made the world. All nations now know the secret kept from many ages; this mystery is manifested in revelation through Jesus Christ. We keep the commandments of God and walk in the obedience of faith eternally. The Saints stand in great numbers, and march into the gates of the Kingdom. In the holy city we decree seventy weeks to end sin and atone iniquities sealing up the vision. Finding favor we are accepted in the covenant that gives restoration to our land, and we receive our inheritance.

We understand that things will be difficult, due to the selfishness of men. Those who love money, and boasting, who are arrogant and unholy haters of God, them who love the pleasures of the world, we avoid. The wicked will not understand and be enraged when many are cleansed, purged, and sanctified. Turning away from deceit and evil sayings, we embrace our faith and duties. We see the betrayals and the hate, man tries to enforce law and order, and hearts grow cold.

This is the last hour in which we must examine ourselves and align our minds in Christ, we know the voice of God and a stranger voice we disregard. The mockers are known to follow their own lustful desires, carrying on as if the promise of His return is slow to come. But we know that the Lord will return as a thief in the night. So then, the Angels will come forth and remove the wicked from the righteous in the end. The heavens pass away with roaring thunders, and sweltering heat destroys the elements as fire destroys the world. We are not of this world but in it as this process refines us as golden without burn.

Raised up with Christ we seek after the things from above, our minds are always set on Him and never man who will fail us. The things of the earth are not permanent or of any importance, but the things of heaven are forever.   Rising in Him, our hidden life awakens, we will be revealed with Him in glory. We encourage each other, and unify, with uplifting words we show our love for each other and do acts of charity. As Jesus said, He is the bread of life; he who comes to Him will not hunger, and he who believes will never thirst. Some of those who saw Him did not believe, but those of us who do believe are from God. We do not deny Christ by now showing His attributes, and He will not cast us out. As Jesus went about doing the will of God over His own will, so must we. Nothing is lost in Him, and on the last day we will rise with Him. We look forward to the promise being kept of the new heaven and new earth of righteousness. At the sound of the trumpet, we are found spotless and blameless at peace in our hearts with Christ. Be thankful that He is patient for our benefit, so that none perish, we stay on guard from sin. Growing in His grace and knowledge we give Jesus Christ all of the praise, honor, and glory forever and forever. Amen.

Coming into the Light that is in us through Him that lives within the soul's temple, clearly the visions are shown as twinkling's of eye-opening experiences.

Engulfed in the flame of passion overthrown by desires of imaginative creations, dreams reveal the projection of goal awakening outcomes.

As the night falls on as dark, may we all feel the peace of the Lord. In our slumber while we sleep, I pray the Angels take charge and guard our feet. While the visions roll back our eyes, let the Heavens open and fold back the skies. As a movie of dreams, let us recall the scenes. Before the dawn of day; the rising of the Sun, if our eyes open, we rejoice in prayer as the Chosen Ones.

Praying at all times without cease, the Kingdom has come, Peace!

Let us not hesitate in removing procrastination, idleness, unforgiveness, bitterness, and all anger, we walk by faith into a New World created by the inspiration of love. We speak the truth in love with honor, girdling our tongues we hold steadfast to the word of God in our hearts. Thinking of excellent things worth praising, we lift each other up in the edification of building up character and the Kingdom of Righteousness. The best medicine is a joyful heart and knowing that laughter brings life to our bones we amuse each other with pleasurable gifts of talents. Instead of being anxious for anything, we ask for needs and grant the desires of our hearts. There is nothing too hard for God, we believe in the impossible happening as a result of coming together as one being in the Spirit of Christ Jesus. We can do all things through Christ's strength in us, and at our weakest moments He is strong through submission of our will for His will being done. Rejoicing in hope, being patient in tribulation, and constant in prayer, we look forward to the triumphant day of our Lord's reign on earth. And we know that for those who love God all things work together for good, so we live our days as if it is already done. He lives in us as He lived before, and we do not conform with the ways of this world but fight for the Kingdom to come. Keeping our hearts with all vigilance, for from it flow the springs of life. Forgetting what lies behind, and straining forward to what lies ahead, we overcome the ways of this world as Christ Jesus did for us. He who is in us is greater than he who is in the world, we stand apart and establish the Kingdom in Him through us. We shall look upon the goodness of the LORD in the land of the living, and never taste death! We believe that the things that are seen are transient, but the things that are unseen are eternal. And, we create by faith all those things that have yet to be imagined. Rejoicing always, praying without cease, and giving thanks in all circumstances; we hold on to our faith, for this is the will of God in Christ Jesus for us all. We do not fear, for the Lord is with us. We are not dismayed, for He is our God. He will strengthen us, He will help us, He will uphold us with His righteous right hand. Trusting in the LORD with all our hearts, and not leaning on our own understanding, we acknowledge Him in all our ways, and allow Him to make our paths straight. We long to taste from the cup of living waters, so that the goodness of it shakes our souls into eternal life. The angel of the LORD encamps around those who fear Him and delivers them from all unrighteousness. Rejoicing always, there is no corrupt talk coming out of our mouths, but only such as is good for building up, fitting the occasion, that it may give grace to everybody who hears. Doing all things without grumbling or questioning, we take on a heart of servitude for the least of us. Having a glad heart with a cheerful face, we share the good news of Christ everywhere and take care of His sheep as directed. Taking His yoke upon us, we learn His ways, because He is gentle and lowly in heart, and we will find rest for our souls. Allowing the peace of Christ to rule our hearts, we accept the call to become one body in Him, so that His will be accomplished on earth. We are thankful for the word of God, and its ability to transform our minds through washing for sanctification. Our God is not a God of confusion but of peace, and we have not been given a spirit of fear but of power and a sound mind. No weapon formed against us shall succeed, and we shall confute every tongue that rises against us in judgment. As servants of the Lord we are vindicated by Him, and we claim our inheritance. Being humbled, under His mighty Hand at the proper time, we will be exalted. We are a chosen race, a royal priesthood, a holy nation, a people for His own possession, called that we may proclaim the excellent works of God who brought us out of darkness into His marvelous light. To all of these things we know that, no one can come against what God has established, and through us let His will be done in earth.

Surrounded by a great cloud of witnesses, we lay aside every weight, and the sin that easily traps us, and we run the race before us with endurance, looking only to Jesus Christ Always, the Author and the Finisher of our Faith. As the joy set before Him endured the cross, detesting the shame, sitting at the right hand of the throne of God. Considering what hostility, He tolerated from sinners, so that we would not become weary or discouraged in our souls. We resist bloodshed and strive to live our lives without sin. We remember that we are Children of the

Most High God and submit to the calling on our lives. We do not despise the rebuke of correction from the Lord, because who the Lord loves He chastens. Being received into the Holy Kingdom, as overcomers in Christ dealt with as Sons and Daughters, we accept being disciplined through love, and show our Father God the upmost respect.

Praise be to God if you endure the chastening until the end, God deals with us as His Sons and Daughters, therefore we willingly subject ourselves to the Father of spirits and live. The profit is of great reward, as we partake in His Holiness. The pain we experience now is only temporary, after the teachings of Christ we receive the peaceable fruit of righteousness. So, let us strengthen ourselves, and stay on the straight and narrow path, so that we are all healed as well as our land.

Pursuing peace with everybody, and being holy as Our Father is Holy, we expect to see the Lord. We guard our eyes and ears being careful not to fall short of the glory of the grace of God. We will go to the mountain not fearing the fires to come, the dark pit, and the blackness of night, the sound of trumpet and the voice of words speak attentively, and we are aware. Many cannot endure the commands, the thought of the government on Christ shoulders and love being law makes the devil mad. Walk into the City of God with fear and trembling, work out your salvation this very moment.

The Angels in Heaven are interceding for us, Satan's angels on earth are hiding and mourning. The assembly of the Saints and the church of the firstborn who are registered in heaven, to God the Judge of all, to the spirits of the justified made perfect, to Jesus the Mediator of the New Covenant, and to the blood of sprinkling that speaks of better things than that of Abel. Hear and understand the voice of Our Heavenly Father, do not refuse Him who speaks, and do not turn away from the One who speaks from Heaven. The voice that shakes the earth, thunders the heavens and pierces the soul. Know, that not only this but He is shaking the Heavens foundations. Only what cannot be shaken remains, what we see now disappears and what is not seen becomes real. The Kingdom we have to come cannot be shaken, having grace we serve God reasonably with reverence and godly fear. For Our God is a consuming fire. The fires are coming, we will all stand together for the separation at judgment. Those who remain will go through the fires, and not be burned. We are more than Overcomers in Christ who sent us, no flesh or blood inherits the Kingdom, only the spirit of God that is in us. Let us continue to pray daily for our world, and fight in the battle for Our Lord to Come from this day on. Pressing forward as One People in Christ, we can do all things.

Don't believe it? Just watch! Stay vigilant and be woke at the Right Hour. He is Coming to expose the evil works of the night; let us all be Children of the Day. In Jesus Name, Amen.

The End.